PIGEON IN A
CROSSWALK

Tales of Anxiety and Accidental Glamour

JACK GRAY

Simon & Schuster

New York   London   Toronto   Sydney   New Delhi

Simon & Schuster
1230 Avenue of the Americas
New York, NY 10020

Copyright © 2013 by Jack Gray

First Simon & Schuster hardcover edition February 2013

SIMON & SCHUSTER and colophon are registered trademarks of Simon & Schuster, Inc.

For information about special discounts for bulk purchases, please contact Simon & Schuster Special Sales at 1-866-506-1949 or business@simonandschuster.com.

The Simon & Schuster Speakers Bureau can bring authors to your live event. For more information or to book an event, contact the Simon & Schuster Speakers Bureau at 1-866-248-3049 or visit our website at www.simonspeakers.com.

Designed by Ruth Lee-Mui

Manufactured in the United States of America

10 9 8 7 6 5 4 3 2 1

Library of Congress Cataloging-in-Publication Data
Gray, Jack L.
    Pigeon in a crosswalk : tales of anxiety and accidental glamour / Jack Gray.
— 1st Simon & Schuster hardcover edition.
        pages   cm
1. Gray, Jack L. 2. Television producers and directors—United States—Biography.
    I. Title.
    PN1992.4.G725A3 2013
    791.4502'32092—dc23
    [B]   2012043178
ISBN 978-1-4516-4134-9
ISBN 978-1-4516-4136-3 (ebook)

For my mother, Maria

CONTENTS

PIGEON IN A

CROSSWALK

FUN WITH A
USED CAMCORDER

The meteorologist was ruining my newscast. She was cranky, unfocused, and, for a seasoned television personality, she spent a lot of time chewing on her barrette. Willard Scott would never pull this shit. It served me right for working with my eight-year-old sister. Even on the rare occasion when she delivered her weather report on cue, she mumbled so much that no one could understand her. She was like Bob Dylan, if Bob Dylan wore saddle shoes and had maternal separation anxiety.

At the time it seemed that my sister, Rose, existed for the sole purpose of driving me crazy. I think I was the only ten-year-old who walked around with a stress ball. She was like a mental patient with an army of Cabbage Patch dolls, just waiting to tattle on me for something minor, like spilling a cup of milk or telling her she was left as an infant on our doorstep in an empty

Doritos bag. I remember once she broke her collarbone. It always had to be about her. And the way she monopolized our mother's time. Surely the woman had more important things to do than to teach my sister how to read. I was waiting for cookies, for fuck's sake.

As it happens, I was stuck with Rose, as both a sibling and a television colleague. There was a shortage of fake meteorologists willing to be paid in grape Pez. It didn't matter, though. I was the star of the show, the founder of the entire network. It was called BNN—Barnstead News Network; Barnstead being the name of the lakeside New Hampshire town in which my maternal grandparents—whose living room housed our "studio"—resided. We had a rudimentary set. The sofa doubled as the anchor desk, our tripod was crooked and the reading lamp hardly matched the crisp glow that bathed Jane Pauley on the *Today* show each morning. But we made do, no doubt thanks to my unflappable leadership. Like any good ten-year-old TV anchor, on the days when my sister refused to provide our viewers with accurate meteorological data, I brought in our backup correspondent, our six-year-old cousin Krista. Granted, she preferred to do her reports while hanging upside down off of the sofa but, still, they had a certain style. A style that has evolved over the subsequent years with an emphasis on makeup and hair extensions, with Krista now exemplifying the downside of what happens when the word "Kardashian" enters the cultural lexicon.

The crucial piece of BNN was, obviously, the video camera itself. A VHS camcorder, it was purchased used by my grandfather Papou. A modern man who passed on to me his love of photography and gadgets, Papou retained his parents' old-world sensibilities and disregard for U.S. law. "What do you mean," he asked me when I was eleven, "you don't know how to *drive*?"

Equal parts savvy consumer and hearty outdoorsman, he was—and remains—as comfortable shopping for preowned electronics as he was euthanizing a turtle caught in my fishing tackle. Frankly, if his lakeside activities were any indication, I think Papou—a medical doctor—might have harbored some regret over never going the Dr. Kevorkian route. To this day I've not met anyone more eager to chloroform marine life.

Then again, I'm not sure I ever quite figured him out. I mean, I once bought him salt and pepper shakers in the shape of toilets and he actually used them. What does *that* say about him? That he likes to humor his grandchildren? Please. The man is clearly a mess. And if that doesn't convince you, consider this: He once came home with a remote-controlled flatulence simulator called Le Farteur. "But it's French!" he protested as my grandmother kicked him into the basement.

One of my most frequent interview subjects on BNN was my great-grandmother. She would come up from Connecticut each summer for a vacation. And by vacation I mean my grandmother and her sisters would take turns passing their mother around among themselves like a plate of baklava. Questionable elder care notwithstanding, I was always glad to see my Yiayia. A Greek immigrant in her nineties, she measured approximately three feet by three feet, never wore anything other than a muumuu, and was obsessed with two things: the soap opera *Guiding Light* and death. No matter what question I posed, her broken English was always the same: "I don't understand why The God don't take me now." Between the two of us, we were one bottle of ouzo away from a murder-suicide pact. For the better part of twenty-five years I was told on an annual basis, "You'd better make sure you visit Yiayia this summer because this might be the last time you see her." That she pleaded constantly for death and ended up living to 103 only further confused my already skewed view of mortality.

Yearly interviews with Yiayia aside, our production schedule at BNN was anything but consistent, though we were always on call for breaking news. One summer a particularly nasty thunderstorm blew through town. (I use the word "town" loosely; it was more of a state highway with a gas station.) I tried to capture dramatic footage by pointing the camera outside but, alas, my grandmother's complex window treatments got in the way. There were blinds, cranks, pulleys, and screens; the windows offered everything except natural light and ventilation.

Without fail, Rose and Krista would tire of my demands and abandon me in the BNN studios. They'd head out to my grandparents' driveway to play hopscotch or sell drugs, it was such a fine line in those days, while I stayed inside, devoted to my burgeoning craft and talking to myself. I grew skilled at doing my own introductions. "And now, your host, Jack Gray," I would boom in a deep voice, off-camera. Walking into the shot, I would thank the imaginary audience, sit down, and launch into a rambling monologue. In retrospect, it was probably closer to an al-Qaeda video than a newscast.

As any good anchorman knows, you can't stay in the studio all the time. You have to get out into the field and talk to folks. I would remove the video camera from the tripod and head into the real world, or my grandmother's kitchen, whichever I came across first. My grandmother, the daughter of my death-obsessed great-grandmother, and whom I also call Yiayia, is one of those remarkable women who doesn't sleep more than ninety minutes a night, always has a warm plate of blueberry muffins on the counter, and will cut a bitch if she misses *Jeopardy*. Look, I'm not saying my grandmother has a crush on Alex Trebek. I'm just saying she used to shout out some pretty filthy answers. Yiayia was camera-shy back then. She wasn't so much interested in being interviewed by me as she was blasting an Elton John CD on the stereo. You haven't lived until you've seen a sixty-year-old woman wearing a New England Patriots t-shirt dance alone to "I'm Still Standing." I was young; I wasn't clear about what I was watching. I just knew it was shame-based.

When Yiayia inevitably pushed me out of the kitchen so she could "get dinner ready" (code for make obscene calls to Alex Trebek), I would go in search of the one member of the family I knew would cooperate. Her name was Abby, a beautiful German shepherd. Broad-shouldered, good-humored, with a gorgeous mane of hair, she was a canine Bea Arthur. I would find Abby—usually down in the basement playing solitaire—and turn on the camera. So serene. Nothing you could do would fluster her. I would point the camera at Abby and ask her questions, "How was your day?" "Did you spot any squirrels around the property?" "Do I look fat in these pants?" The usual journalist-dog conversation. She would just kind of nod. One of those slight moves of the head that could have been either a signal of recognition or, as it often was with Bea Arthur, just gas. Then I would lie down next to her and snuggle up for a bit. Granted, that's kind of an ethical gray area for a reporter. But you can't tell me that Barbara Walters didn't do the same thing with Fidel Castro. Abby would sigh and give me a couple licks across the top of my head, and then we would go out and play for a while, leaving the camcorder behind. Just a dog and his anchorman.

The BNN tapes still exist. There's a trove of VHS cassettes somewhere in my grandparents' basement, probably near the shoebox full of my grandmother's unsuccessful horse track betting slips. My grandfather keeps saying he's going to transfer the tapes to DVDs. Everyone knows that will never happen. His days as a technology pioneer are over. He'd probably transfer the VHS cassettes to silent film reels. When I was young, on the way to my grandparents' house, I would daydream about what new and exciting electronic gadget Papou would have to show me. Now I realize it's the other way around. He asks me about my phone and my camera and, when I hand them over to him, he does that maneuver senior citizens do where they take off their glasses and hold an item at arm's length, examining it suspiciously. I considered buying him an iPad for his birthday, but then I remembered that he's too old and I'm too cheap.

It's just as well that those tapes are collecting dust. What would I want to do, watch them? No, thanks. Should I ever want to be embarrassed by what I say or how I look, I have access to clips of my occasional CNN appearances. I wonder if my grandparents ever thought, when I was making those BNN tapes in their house all those years ago, that I would ever make a living in the television business. Probably not. They likely just crossed their fingers that I wouldn't become a drug addict or get anyone pregnant—a crapshoot in any family. To some extent, Yiayia and Papou still think of me as the little boy with the camcorder, barking out orders to his sister and cousin. When I gave my grandmother a tour of CNN, she took me aside and whispered, "Do you think Anderson Cooper would want to watch those BNN tapes? I should ask him." I could feel the blood draining from my face.

"No, that's alright," I said, "his VCR is broken."

"Oh, really? That's a shame."

"Yeah, don't even mention it to him, he's quite upset about it."

And then we walked into the television studio. A real television studio.

NOBODY CALLS IT BEANTOWN

Benazir Bhutto needed directions to Best Buy. Her children wanted a DVD of the new Jim Carrey movie *Lemony Snicket's A Series of Unfortunate Events,* and she'd promised she'd get it for them on her trip to Boston. The former prime minister of Pakistan was waiting in the makeshift green room at New England Cable News, where I produced a nightly news and interview program. She requested a cup of tea, which I said I'd get, not mentioning that I was a moron and didn't know how to make tea. I got more than a few strange looks when I ran through the newsroom shouting, "Help! Benazir Bhutto wants some Earl Grey!" Working in local news, you're much more likely to instead hear things like "There's a three-alarm fire downtown," or "The meteorologist is crying again."

At first I hadn't even expected to "book" Bhutto. I'd heard

she was coming to Boston to deliver a speech at a Simmons College event, so I reached out through an intermediary. To my surprise, she accepted the invitation. I'd never heard of a world leader sitting for an in-depth interview on a local news program that also includes the phrase "now let's get a check of the five-day forecast." I would need to provide transportation for her, I was told. It was not an unusual request for most guests, though I was a bit surprised that a former head of state—especially one as controversial as Bhutto—wouldn't have her own driver and security. Then again, at the time, she was living in relatively peaceful exile in Dubai and London. Perhaps there was nothing to worry about. I called the limo company we used and booked the biggest SUV they had, figuring she would be traveling with an entourage. I crossed my fingers that the car service would show up, punctuality not being its specialty. I also specified that SUV meant SUV. I once booked a sedan to pick up former New Hampshire Governor Jeanne Shaheen and they dispatched one of those white stretch limos only appropriate for proms and mob weddings.

The Bhutto booking was a milestone for me at New England Cable News (NECN). I had come a long way since my first week, when one of my assignments was to input the winning lottery numbers into the Chyron machine that displayed them on-air. Well, you know how some people can be sticklers for details? It turns out I aired the wrong numbers. I mean, really, was that such a big deal? Sure some poor guy watching thought he won and ran down to his local convenience store to celebrate, only to be told that his ticket wasn't even worth the paper it was printed on. I get that he was disappointed, but let's not lose sight of the fact that by calling the station to complain, he cut into my dinner break. Besides, the lotto snafu was nothing compared to the station's most legendary blooper that, unfortunately, happened before my time.

The anchor, as legend goes, was reading what's called a "tease," which is the last thing viewers see and hear before a commercial break. On this particular night the tease was written with the intention of getting viewers to stick around for a story about the arrival of the Rockefeller Center Christmas tree. The script was written, "Coming up, how'd you like to have to string the lights on this baby?" The script also called for a brief video clip of the tree. So, the time comes for the commercial break, the theme music begins to play, and the anchor says, "Coming up, how'd you like to have to string the lights on this baby?" Except the video they showed wasn't of the Rockefeller Center Christmas tree. The video was of Mother Teresa. On a stretcher.

When I was growing up in suburban Boston, my idol was a man named Chet Curtis. He and his then wife and coanchor, Natalie Jacobson, reigned for decades as the most popular and highest-rated anchor team in Massachusetts. They were the Brad and Angelina of local news, except not as pouty. To this day, long after their public and private split, Chet and Nat are still household names in New England. I got to know them each a bit when I interned in the summer of 2000 at WCVB-TV, the ABC affiliate known simply as Channel 5. "Got to know them" is a bit of a stretch. "Faked needed to use the Xerox machine so I could walk past them" would be more accurate.

Nothing lasts forever, especially in television. I was sad to read in 2001 that Chet was leaving Channel 5, but I was also excited that he would be moving to NECN, also based in Metro Boston. I wanted a job there after I graduated from college, which in and of itself was a long shot unless my school awarded degrees in borderline nervous breakdowns.

They say that mental illness, if it presents itself, tends to show up first when one is college-aged. Like clockwork, depression set in, with a sidecar of mild obsessive-compulsive disorder, my senior year. I checked light switches, I checked the stove, I counted things over and over and over. Mostly I was just sad. My future was, at best, unclear. I quit my job at the campus radio station and went through the motions of my final semester. All around me, my classmates were reveling in excitement and possibility. We were twenty-one, and when you're twenty-one, you're everything. Sometimes I cried, sometimes I panicked, most of the time I slept. I lost weight. I moved to my mother's house, where I padded around in my pajamas, like some J. Crew version of Howard Hughes. My mother saved my life. She took me to get help, and I found relief in psychiatrists and antidepressants. I pulled back from the abyss. Somehow I managed to graduate. College almost killed me, but at least I looked slim in my commencement photo.

Incredibly, I got a job at NECN. I was hired as a freelance weekend production assistant, which is about as entry-level as you can get in the television news business. I love recent college graduates who complain about their full-time, Monday-through-Friday, 9 A.M.-to-5 P.M. jobs, complete with health insurance, paid time off, and a 401k retirement plan. "Well, it's entry-level, but better than nothing." Go fuck yourselves.

For the first few months after graduation I split my time working at both NECN and New Hampshire Public Television, about eighty miles to the north. I lived with my mother and drove between my two jobs in a used Nissan with a ceiling stained with root beer and cigarette ashes. I didn't care. I was happy just to be working in my chosen profession.

After a few weeks at NECN, I started to feel like I had a purpose. I was way too low on the station ladder to work with Chet, and I was still broke and mired in credit card debt, but I was getting paid to work in television. Eventually a full-time job opened up and I was hired. I said goodbye to my hours at New Hampshire Public Television—a fine channel, even though in all my time there I never got one lousy PBS tote bag.

My duties as a production assistant at NECN were to do whatever the newscast producer wanted. That usually included choosing sound bites or writing scripts for the less important voice-overs the anchor would read. My duties, I soon learned, apparently also included showing up on time, which was not one of my strengths. By fall I had moved into an apartment in Boston. My 10 A.M. start time conflicted with my habit of going to 7-Eleven at 3 A.M. to buy scratch tickets and day-old doughnuts and then returning to my apartment and climbing into bed with a vial of Prozac, a glass of red wine, and a VHS cassette of *Fletch*. That might not be in the *Physicians' Desk Reference* under "insomnia remedies" but it worked for me. It took, however, only one comment from a superior and I got the message: punctuality was not optional. That's not to say I didn't still go out at night, but I made damn sure I was at work on time, even on the dreadful morning I drove back from Foxwoods Casino after losing my rent money in an all-night roulette binge. Nothing illustrates the glamour of a gambling addiction quite like searching your backseat for loose change on a Tuesday morning outside a Dunkin' Donuts in Connecticut.

Producing local television news isn't necessarily easy, but it's not necessarily tough. Either way it played to my skill set, and I was eventually promoted to newscast producer, responsible for the noon and 4 P.M. shows. The noon anchors also did the early-morning news, so by the time they got to me, they were done. Just fucking done. I was the last person they wanted to hear chime in with "fresh" angles on stories they'd been reporting on all morning. That's not to say they weren't nice. They were, when they weren't making me cry. I preferred my 4 P.M. anchor. One night she offered to pay for dinner if I'd go out to McDonald's and pick up the food. Her order was two 10-piece servings of Chicken McNuggets, two large fries, and a large Coke. Where had *this* lady been all my life? I got the same thing. Turns out, she was three months pregnant. I wasn't sure of my excuse.

The producers all sat in desks organized in what was called a pod, at a time when that word wasn't trendy but just weird. Against my better judgment I made friends with many of my coworkers. We laughed during our shifts and hung out in our free time. I even lived with one of my colleagues for two years. It turned out my concerns about mixing work and pleasure were misplaced. There's something wonderful about being able to call your roommate upon pulling into the television station parking lot and saying, "Can you bring me a clean pair of boxer shorts? I just did that thing where I tried to fart but instead I shit myself."

That wasn't the only benefit of being friends with your colleagues, though, let's face it, that was a big one. We drank on weekends and went to each other's parties, we shoveled each other out after blizzards, and smoked pot and watched the sunrise after the final night of the Democratic National Convention. It was like college, only I wasn't in the fetal position weeping.

I did the noon and the four o'clock shows for a year or so, and I did a weekend stint, too, and filled in on some overnight shifts. I did whatever I could to impress management and, hopefully, move one step closer to working in prime time with the legendary Chet Curtis. One day my bosses approached me to see if I'd be interested in producing a new, nightly 8 P.M. show called *The Chet Curtis Report*. Hell, yes, I would. The creative vision for the new show was vague, which I loved. Chet and I would be able to build it pretty much however we wanted. That meant not only a conventional news component, but also the creative freedom to book guests from politics and show business. I had visions of a hybrid Boston newscast–*Cheers* reunion with Shelley Long sitting on Chet's lap while they narrated live coverage of a car chase.

Chet was among the last of the old guard of local-news titans, from an era when anchors spent their careers in one place and knew the people and communities they reported on. He was paid handsomely for it, too. The Mercedes, the plane he piloted himself, the boat, the waterfront homes. There was a saying around NECN: "It's good to be Chet." But a more generous man I have never met. He never let anyone else pick up a tab. He treated me to more meals than I can recall. And I'm not the cheapest date, either. I head straight for the wine menu.

And yet, as much as he lived the golden life, I could not have asked for a more unpretentious mentor. Chet was the most gregarious guy in the newsroom. He knew everyone's name and always said hello, no matter your job. All he ever asked of anyone was a Red Sox score and a light for his Marlboro. We were a great team. We were so close that, according to me, I was the son he never had. And not only did we get along, he gave me the kind of professional latitude that only someone entirely secure in his career can give. He knew I would fuck up, but he was willing to take the chance. And from time to time, I did fuck up. Like the night I was talking into Chet's earpiece during the weather segment. "He's so full of shit," I said, referring to our meteorologist who was currently on live television, "It's not going to fucking rain tomorrow. He's been wrong all week. What the hell is he smoking anyway?" It turned out I had pressed the wrong button and was talking into the meteorologist's earpiece.

Aborted forecasts aside, I had near-complete control over all aspects of our show, from the stories we covered in the hard news block to the lengthy celebrity and newsmaker interviews we did in the second half of the program. I managed to book some big names: from Massachusetts politicians like Governor Mitt Romney and Senator John Kerry to visiting dignitaries like House Minority Leader Nancy Pelosi and Senator Joe Biden. I even got Secretary of State Condoleezza Rice, though only after agreeing to pay $300 for a professional makeup artist. For a national television network, that's nothing. But in local news, I might as well have asked my boss for a kidney.

There were plenty of bookings I didn't get. I always tried, though. Well, almost always. One sensational opportunity presented itself on a summer morning in 2005. It started with jury duty, my first time, in downtown Boston. There was a woman in the back row—blond hair, big sunglasses, and a scarf around her head. Glamorous and familiar looking, if a bit rough around the edges. Holy shit, I thought, it's Joan Kennedy. One of Boston's most famous residents, the ex-wife of Senator Ted Kennedy lived a quiet life in the city's Back Bay neighborhood as a socialite and arts patron. Sadly, she'd also become one of Boston's best-known recovering, and struggling, alcoholics.

A few months prior she had been found unconscious on a sidewalk. It was all over the news. The whole thing was a mess. Most of us were just waiting around in the jury room, but no food was allowed in there so some people were eating outside in the hallway. I left to find a restroom (and by restroom I mean vending machine), and when I returned I saw Mrs. Kennedy sitting on the floor—there were no benches in the hallway—having a snack. The woman who lived through the assassinations of two brothers-in-law, who stood by her husband after Chappaquiddick, who once upon a time had been a great beauty and who would have been First Lady of the United States had Senator Kennedy won the 1980 presidential election, did not look well.

Fascinated and saddened by what I saw, I was curious to talk to her, though I didn't have the nerve to intrude. Before I could consider the situation further, the clerk dismissed us from jury service. Everyone rushed for the elevators, and I found myself in the same one as Mrs. Kennedy. I thought of asking her to sit down for an interview with Chet. What a huge "get" that would be. But, once again, as much as I wanted to say something, I couldn't. I just didn't have that Barbara Walters instinct. Barbara would have thrown Joan Kennedy over her shoulder, tossed her in a van, and made a beeline for *The View*.

I walked out of the courthouse. That's that, I thought. But then I had to look back. I don't know why, but I did. And Mrs.

Kennedy was clearly disoriented. She walked in one direction, then back the other way. *Jesus Christ, here we go.* "Mrs. Kennedy," I said as I approached her, "you don't know me, but we have a mutual acquaintance, Chet Curtis." (Chet had known the Kennedy family, personally and professionally, for years.) Her eyes flashed with recognition. "Oh yes," she said, smiling.

"I noticed we were in the same jury pool and I was just wondering if you were all set getting home," I said.

"To tell you the truth, I was going to walk home but I'm not quite sure how to get there from here." *Jesus.* It was probably 85 degrees, she was almost seventy years old and at least thirty minutes away from her home by foot. "Well, I have a car if you want a ride," I said. If my mother were in a similar situation, I would hope that someone would assist her. At least that's how I rationalized it to myself. But I know deep down the journalist in me was too curious to just let her wander away into the morning without having a conversation.

"Oh, that'd be wonderful, are you sure you don't mind?" she said.

"Not at all," I said, and off we went, walking through Government Center in downtown Boston toward the parking garage where I'd left my dinged-up Honda Accord. Heads turned as we passed. I felt like I'd smoked a bad joint rolled from a page in an American history textbook.

We walked into the garage. My car was missing. *You've got to be fucking kidding me.* I was sure we were in the right garage. At least I thought I was sure. If you've ever experienced the frustration of wandering around a parking garage looking for your car, imagine doing it with Joan Kennedy trailing behind you. Fortunately she was kind of oblivious that day. Anyone who was "all there" would have surely panicked and thought I was leading them off to be murdered. We found my car obscured behind a van. Mrs. Kennedy noticed I had New Hampshire license plates. It used to be my mother's car, I explained, and I hadn't gotten around to changing them. As we pulled out of the garage, she said, "Well, you know, I'm originally a Bennett and the Bennetts spent time in New Hampshire when they first came to this country." And then, in a moment that felt like an outtake from some kind of insane miniseries, she turned to me and said, "In fact, you know, the Bennetts were over here long before the Kennedys. The Kennedys were still in Ireland rolling around in mud with the pigs." Well, helllllo there, Joan. Care to go on record with that one? Keep in mind I hadn't even paid the parking lot attendant before she'd broken out that little nugget. The lady sure knew how to deliver an opener.

As we drove through Beacon Hill, Mrs. Kennedy proceeded to tell me how her children encouraged her to work on some genealogy projects. I didn't dare bring up that these were the children who had been all over the newspapers as they sought to control their mother's finances and health care. She also said she was planning on driving down to the Cape for the July 4th weekend. I couldn't imagine she was allowed to operate a motor vehicle under any circumstances, but I let that one slide, too. "But, you know, I've made some fascinating discoveries," she said, back on the topic of genealogy. "Some of my relatives were burned at the stake during the Salem Witch Trials. And do you know why?" she asked.

"No," I said, not having a good feeling about where this was going.

"They burned them alive because they were women's

libbers!" she said. And then she hit me. Not hard, but she reached over and smacked my arm, as a way of underscoring her point. "Isn't that fun?" she said. "Isn't that fun?" she said again.

Just get me out of here, I thought. There has to be a law in Massachusetts against driving around with a Kennedy and letting them say crazy shit and smack you.

The ride, thankfully, was nearing its end. Mrs. Kennedy directed me to her condominium building on Beacon Street. I stopped the car by the curb and took one last look at her. Age, combined with alcoholism and the strain of what by all accounts had not been an easy life, had weathered Joan Bennett Kennedy. But there was still an inkling of how stunning she once was; "The dish," her brother-in-law President John F. Kennedy reportedly called her. "Are you all set getting inside?" I asked. "Yup," she said, pausing a beat and looking at me, almost as if she wasn't sure why she was in my car—which made two of us. "Thanks! Bye!" she exclaimed with a big smile on her face. And then she was gone. I never did ask her to be on our show.

Meeting Ted Kennedy was a different experience. The first time I saw him in person was the summer of 1994, a dozen years after he and Joan divorced. I was at the Yankee Homecoming Parade in Newburyport, Massachusetts, a few miles from where I grew up. At the time, the senator was locked in a tough reelection bid against a little-known businessman named Mitt Romney, whom I also met that day. From my perch on the sidewalk, I heard the crowd down the street start to cheer. And then I saw him. The giant, famous face, the wavy hair, the one-size-too-small polo shirt. And then I heard the voice—that inimitable sound, the Canada goose of American politics. He bounded—and yes, those were the days when he could still bound—down the street with his beautiful new wife, Vicki, in tow, shaking hands and greeting the crowds. For a teenage news junkie like me, shaking the hand of the man whom I had read about and watched on television for years was a life-changing experience.

It electrified my interest in politics and journalism. It was also an experience that I made the mistake of telling my grandfather about as soon as I got home. He hated Ted Kennedy. "Did you meet Mary Jo Kopechne, too?" he hollered. "Oh, that's right, you didn't, because Ted Kennedy killed her." Good old Bumpy, never one to pass up an opportunity to leave an emotional scar. When I got older, whenever my grandfather would go on one of his rants about how liberals were so terrible, I would just switch the wallpaper on his computer to a picture of Jane Fonda in Vietnam and get the hell out of there.

In the years following that day at the parade, I met Senator Kennedy a dozen or so times. Most of those meetings were because of TV interviews I produced, others were by chance. There was the time I was walking through Boston with my mother and sister during my freshman year of college when we came upon the senator standing alone on the sidewalk outside his townhouse on Marlborough Street, soaking up the sun—kind of like a turtle—waiting for Vicki to join him. He was, as was his way, gracious when we stopped to talk with him for a few minutes. He and Vicki were headed, he said, to one of his nephews' soccer games. There's a lot people can say about Ted Kennedy, but they can't say he wasn't dedicated to his family. He would often arrive at interviews with a supersized Kennedy entourage: his wife, his in-laws, his nephews, even his two Portuguese water dogs, Sunny and Splash. And, yes, as my grandfather pointed out to me, Splash may have been a poor choice for a name.

Despite his being one of the most famous politicians in America, I never had trouble booking Senator Kennedy to do interviews with Chet. From an in-depth taping in a Fenway Park skybox—during which the senator looked over at me, his nephews, and his dogs and told us all to basically shut the fuck up—to a vibrant in-studio discussion about partisan Washington vitriol, Curtis and Kennedy hashed out local and national policy in a way you didn't see anywhere else on local television in Boston. Chet even moderated Ted Kennedy's final televised debate with a campaign opponent, which I produced. In the green room that day, just as I was leading him out the door toward the studio, the senator asked me, referring to his Republican challenger, "Now what's this fella's name again?" Everyone froze for a moment until he winked and broke into a wide, mischievous grin.

The trust and chemistry between Chet and the senator made sense. They'd known each other for decades. Chet, a young Washington reporter at the time, was in the U.S. Senate gallery on November 22, 1963, when a staffer rushed to Kennedy's side and said, "Senator, your brother the president has been shot." Unlike his brothers, Ted Kennedy lived to see the twilight of his life. After one interview we did with him, which happened to fall on the senator's seventy-fourth birthday, we had a small celebration for him in the studio. I handed him a big piece of cake decorated with an American flag. The paper plate was flimsy and his hands were shaking. I brought over several more plates

to put underneath and steady things up. And I stood there, with Chet Curtis and Ted Kennedy, as the senator ate his birthday cake and got frosting on the side of his mouth.

It took a while, but I figured out how to make Benazir Bhutto a cup of tea. I have no idea if she ever made it to Best Buy to pick up that DVD for her children. The interview went well. It was everything I had hoped it'd be—compelling, substantive, and relevant. Not bad for a local show. The former prime minister made it clear that returning to Pakistan, despite the dangers she would face, was a priority. At the time it all seemed so abstract. She seemed much more of a pundit-in-exile than someone who would return to the volatile political climate of Pakistan. But she did, and in December 2007, she was assassinated.

My phone rang on a Saturday. It was Chet. "Wanna take a spin in the plane?" he asked. "Let me check my schedule," I joked, because nothing is funnier than a sixty-five-year-old laughing at you for having no life. "OK, meet me at Hanscom Field in an hour," he said. It would be my first time going up in his single-engine Beechcraft Bonanza. Chet had been flying for decades. I was nonchalant about going up with him, but still, what if the engine conked out? Who would save the flight attendants? There were flight attendants, right? In the hangar that afternoon I watched as he prepped the plane for takeoff, which unfortunately did not involve a preflight glass of Chardonnay. I had no idea what he was doing but was relieved that I did not hear the phrase "Hopefully that will be enough gas." As we lifted

off from Hanscom, he said, "Let me know if you see any planes coming toward us." *Me* let him know?! What about the tower?! Didn't they still have towers?! We headed south, past Metro Boston and the South Shore, over Cape Cod and out toward Martha's Vineyard and Nantucket. I didn't say much. I just kind of stared out the cockpit window, trying to absorb the view and—of course—keep an eye out for errant aircraft. By the time we circled back and headed north, I had relaxed to the point where I could consider my good fortune. Not only had I grown up to work with my idol, not only had we become friends, but now I was in his plane. Even though I was the copilot from hell, it was still incredible. Naturally, Chet put the perfect cap on my little moment of bliss by saying, as we passed over the Pilgrim Nuclear Power Station in Plymouth, "How close do you think we can get before they shoot us down?"

As we returned to Hanscom, he told me he wanted me to keep in mind a famous old pilot quote: "Any landing you can walk away from is a good landing." It's now been a long time since I worked with Chet. I see him maybe twice a year. He sold the Beechcraft Bonanza a few years ago. But to this day whenever I'm on a plane and the wheels touch down, I think of him.

Every time.

GOD SAVE THIS
HONORABLE COFFEE

I was lucky I didn't get shot. It was late one night in 2005 and I had slowed my Honda Accord to a near halt outside the home of United States Supreme Court Justice Stephen Breyer. This was before the era of widespread vehicle navigation systems. Not only was I loitering in front of his house, I had my interior dome light on while I fiddled with a printout of MapQuest street directions. To Justice Breyer, or any of his neighbors observing me from a distance, the situation would have appeared beyond suspicious. It would have looked as if I were playing with, at worst, a weapon or, at best, myself.

It wasn't the first time a member of my family had been on the brink of an awkward encounter with a member of the nation's highest court. My grandmother once shadowed David Souter in the fish section of a New Hampshire grocery store. At the time, Justice Souter was a major local celebrity who, in his free time, apparently enjoyed a nice piece of haddock, and my grandmother was, well, let's just say, a serious connoisseur of cooking sherry, if you know what I mean.

As for me, I was supposed to be at Justice Breyer's house. I had been invited. Well, technically, the invitation was for about twelve hours later, but I was hoping the Supreme Court's motto was "Eh, close enough." All I was doing that night was scoping out the precise location of his Cambridge, Massachusetts, home to make sure I could find it the following morning when I arrived to produce a rare sit-down television interview with the justice for NECN. And, if there was time left over, steal a tie and sniff his furniture.

I was worried that if I didn't scout the route to Justice Breyer's house we might get lost and delayed, and even miss out on the interview altogether. Not only would my job at NECN end, my dream of becoming best friends with Ruth Bader Ginsburg would end as well. (You're crazy if you think I was going to leave that house without her e-mail address, or at least information on where she got her eyeglass frames.) It all felt so tenuous because the booking was such a long shot in the first place. Members of the Supreme Court are press-shy, seldom giving interviews, certainly not to local television stations. So when I read that Justice Breyer had written a book called *Active Liberty,* I figured if I ever had a chance of securing an interview with one of the nine brethren, that was it. Unfortunately the publicity department at Justice Breyer's publisher, Knopf, had no interest in my interview request. The justice was doing interviews with Larry King and C-SPAN's Brian Lamb, and that was it.

Disappointed but not vanquished, I made an "emergency" request directly to the Supreme Court. Well, it was an "emergency" from my perspective. The Court, apparently, has more important matters that fall into that category. But I laid out my case of why Justice Breyer should do our interview. I stressed that as a former Harvard Law School professor and federal judge in Massachusetts, he would be familiar with my anchorman, Chet Curtis. Chet was thrilled I was pursuing Breyer. He followed the Court and knew it would be an absorbing discussion. Still, just in case he and Breyer hit it off and started joking around, I warned him to get any ribald limericks about Sandra Day O'Connor out of his system beforehand.

I wasn't sure if I'd ever hear back from the Supreme Court or if my interview request went off into some black hole. Maybe Justice Scalia ate it. Then, one day, I was on my way to work and had stopped, as I always did, for frozen yogurt at White Mountain Creamery on Commonwealth Avenue in Chestnut Hill, across the street from Boston College. Society is comfortable with frozen yogurt because it sounds healthy. My daily fix was anything but. First of all, I ordered two. Every day. I rationalized the excess by telling myself that single people will never break free of depression and find true love unless they are first able to visualize what their lives will be like with someone else. At the time, my way of doing that was to eat a pile of mint chocolate chip smothered with chocolate sprinkles and a large vanilla with generous portions of peanut butter cups on behalf of both myself and my yet-to-be-determined life partner.

As if that wasn't bad enough, I always ate one of them while I drove my car—which is apparently quite dangerous—because

I was too ashamed to walk into NECN with both. Not only that, my brain is wired in such a way that I cannot eat food while listening to music in a car. So, whether I'm driving with a frozen yogurt on my lap or just sitting in a McDonald's parking lot crying into a pile of hamburger wrappers, I absolutely must be listening to either local news radio or NPR. I have similar issues when I'm at home. When I'm eating tuna salad or macaroni and cheese or spaghetti—the extent of my cooking repertoire—I have to be watching *Seinfeld, I Love Lucy, The Golden Girls,* or *Frasier.* In short, I'm uncomplicated. And, by the way, still single and ready for love.

On that particular day, as I inhaled my vanilla frozen yogurt with peanut butter cups and drove toward work, my phone rang. Once upon a time when I was younger and unaware that I wasn't going to stay stretched out and skinny forever, I could drive a car, eat a hamburger, drink a Coke, smoke a cigarette, and talk on my phone all at the same time, with one leg hanging out the window. But no longer. Stuffed into my seat, it was all I could do to try to avoid spilling the yogurt on my crotch while I reached for the phone. The call was from a 202 area code. It was Kathy Arberg, spokeswoman for the Supreme Court of the United States, calling to say that Justice Breyer had agreed to our interview request, provided we could do it that week. If memory serves I had maybe forty-eight hours to prepare, including reading Justice Breyer's book—not exactly easily digested material—and assembling research for Chet. I also had to schedule a crew, which was never simple at NECN. Local news is a world of fires and inclement weather, not in-depth sit-downs with high-ranking judges. At minimum, a proper field interview with a dignitary requires two cameras. But there was a shortage of crews and I ended up securing only one camera. One camera. For a sitting Supreme Court justice. It was unreal, but there were no other options. His Honor would be accorded the same television treatment as people who watched their neighbor's house burn down.

So, there I sat, in my idling Honda Accord, outside Justice Breyer's house late that night before the interview. At least I thought it was his house. I couldn't see a street number anywhere. I couldn't even see a street sign. I was tempted to just go knock on the door and ask if it was indeed the home of the Honorable Stephen G. Breyer, but I had flashes of me screaming "objection withdrawn" as I tried to outrun a Doberman through the streets of Cambridge. The time for loitering was over. All I could do was hope that I'd found the right neighborhood and that I'd be able to find my way back the next day. I gave the Honda some gas and wondered if my license plate was already on file with Homeland Security.

The next morning, in addition to my MapQuest directions, Chet and I were also armed with the justice's private home phone number, provided by the Supreme Court spokeswoman in case we got lost. Don't think I didn't keep that phone number. Who wouldn't? I had this idea in my head that if I ever got caught shoplifting Parmesan cheese from Whole Foods—which could easily happen on one of my darker days—I would call up Stephen Breyer and he'd have me released. "Jack, you rascal," he'd say as he signed the paperwork, "just for this, the next two dinners are on you." As it happens, not only did I save his phone number, I accidentally memorized it. I couldn't help it. It was just one of those things that you look at and you're like, "Holy shit, I'm not supposed to have this information," and you automatically tattoo it onto your brain. I did the same thing with Leonardo DiCaprio's e-mail address. I mean, under no circumstances should I have Leonardo DiCaprio's e-mail address. But I was in Los Angeles and a friend was showing me something on her computer and I couldn't help seeing that her e-mail was open and, well, you know how it is when you're glancing at a friend's e-mail and they just happen to have a message from Leonardo DiCaprio.

Chet had a cigarette or three as we drove to the interview. He's one of the greatest people I've ever met, but he couldn't give a shit about filling your car up with smoke. I remember the first time he did it. He didn't even ask. He just gave me a look that said, "Shut up, it's a fucking Honda." I remembered, turn for turn, exactly how I'd gotten to the justice's neighborhood the night before. When Chet asked me how I was so sure of where we were going, I told him that I'd scouted the property in the dead of night. By the look on his face I might as well have told him I was Son of Sam.

We arrived in Justice Breyer's neighborhood and parked the car outside what I hoped was his house. I figured an aide or housekeeper would be waiting for us, but when we rang the doorbell, the justice himself appeared. Just like that. One of the most powerful people in the United States, answering the door like June Cleaver. Meeting a figure of such achievement and gravitas would prove to be, for a long time, difficult to top. Yes, years later I would meet Gene Hackman and that would cause me to reevaluate everything, but I imagine Gene Hackman has that effect on a lot of gay twenty-nine-year-olds. Still, when it comes to the test of time, having a conversation with a Supreme

Court justice inside his own home beats interrupting a book signing by shouting out lines from *Hoosiers*.

Justice Breyer was gracious. He made us and our crew—the solitary cameraman that NECN had allotted me—feel welcome. The nice thing about interviewing someone who so seldom speaks to the news media is that I don't think he realized just how pathetic it was that we only had one camera. He probably just thought that most field interviews were done that way, with one videographer panning back and forth between the guest and the interviewer, like some low-budget oral history of a deathbed grandparent.

At one point he offered us coffee, which he himself served on a tray. I don't drink coffee, but I wasn't about to decline anything from a Supreme Court justice. So I did what any polite guest would have done: I accepted it with profuse thanks, took a sip, and then, when His Honor wasn't looking, poured the rest down my pants.

We set up in his study, which so perfectly embodied the refuge of a great Cambridge legal mind that it could have been the work of a Hollywood set designer. A large desk, deep chairs, scores of leather-bound books, and windows overlooking the yard. There was even a framed cartoon on the wall that showed one justice saying to another, "Do you ever have one of those days when everything seems unconstitutional?" At one point the justice asked out loud, of no one in particular, "Tie or no tie?" which I found charming. He put on a tie.

As we expected, it was a fascinating interview. Justice Breyer's breadth of knowledge knew no bounds, which, of course, was as it should be. I would hate to leave an interview with a member of the Supreme Court thinking, Yikes, he doesn't seem too bright. You'll rarely get a sitting Supreme Court justice to comment on specific rulings, because there's always a chance the issue will arise again. But he was more than happy to expand on the nuances of legal theory. I know nothing says "riveting local newscast" more than the nuances of legal theory, but I was fortunate to work for a station that valued substance over style. We ended up running the Breyer interview as its own half-hour special edition of *The Chet Curtis Report*. Most local stations would not be interested in such an interview, unless the justice lived next door to a house where a moose had gotten into the backyard pool.

We had three copies of Justice Breyer's book with us. One he signed for Chet. Another, in a shameless attempt to curry favor with my boss, I asked him to sign for the president of our station. And the third, well, it just about killed me to do it, but instead of asking him to inscribe it to me, I asked him to sign it to my father. I knew my dad—a major civics buff—would love it. Plus, I hated the idea of passing up an opportunity to remind my dad that my life was more interesting than his.

I could have stayed in that study all day, listening to the discussion of legal theory and jurisprudence, but once we were done, that was it. The home of a Supreme Court justice is not a place to linger and ask if there is a billiard room. We thanked the justice for his hospitality and said our goodbyes. As we walked to my Honda, I checked my imitation attaché case to make sure I was leaving with everything I'd brought in. Especially the piece of paper with his phone number on it. We got into the car and headed down the street.

"So, what did you think?" I asked Chet.

"Helluva guy. Brilliant. One of the most interesting people I've ever interviewed," he said, pausing as if he had something else to add.

"But?" I said, nervous.

"Can you believe he gave us instant coffee?"

IT'S ALWAYS TRASH NIGHT IN NEW YORK CITY

I had never heard of Glenn Beck. It was November of 2006 and I was sitting in the Time Warner Center office of the head of recruiting for CNN in New York. "He has a show on Headline News," she said, referring to the network's sister channel that was later renamed HLN. "He does a lot of commentary, he's big on radio." It still wasn't registering, though, frankly, unless his show was devoted to powdered Hostess Donettes and the clinically depressed twenty-somethings who eat them by the boxful, I was unlikely to have heard of it. Regardless, it so happened that this Glenn Beck fellow had an opening for a booker; a position for which the recruiter said she could get me an interview. It didn't sound like the kind of job I was looking for, and that was before she uttered what will go down as one of my life's great understatements: "Politically, he's a bit to the right."

I knew I wanted to move to New York, but I didn't have the balls—and by balls I mean money . . . and balls—to do it without a job lined up. From my apartment in Boston, where I was burned out on local news and Dunkin' Donuts, I e-mailed everyone I knew in the television industry, hopeful for a career fairy tale. Surely there was someone who knew someone who knew someone at CNN who loved my résumé and wanted to hire me on the spot as a national television producer. As it turns out, that doesn't happen, at least not to me.

So, I went about my job search the old-fashioned way. No, not sleeping with someone in management; the other old-fashioned way, the way that involves applying with your pants on, which is certainly less fun. Gone were the days of mailing or faxing or even e-mailing résumés to potential employers. Everything went through some monstrous, centralized Web site. You uploaded your cover letter and résumé, and then as far as I was concerned it went directly to Ted Turner's in-box. Sure, Mr. Turner didn't own CNN anymore, but at that point I wasn't letting my fantasies get bogged down by facts.

It was September 11, 2006, a date I noted only after I had submitted my résumé. At the time, I was upset with myself for having not paid attention to the calendar, my logic being that anything submitted to a global news organization on the fifth anniversary of the attacks would be lost in the shuffle. Ted Turner had much more important things to do on 9/11 than peruse my list of college honors. Especially since I had none.

A few days went by. I heard nothing. Then a week. Then

two weeks. A month. Fine, fuck you, Ted Turner. I hope you're enjoying your bison farm while my dreams go unfulfilled. I resigned myself to the reality that CNN just wasn't interested in me. Then on November 11, 2006—two months from the day I submitted my résumé—I received a phone call from someone in the recruiting department at CNN. She had reviewed my résumé, and wondered if I would be available to come to New York to meet with one of her colleagues. As urine gushed down my leg, I explained to her that, yes, I was indeed available to go to New York. "What about this Thursday?" she asked. "Perfect, I actually have Thursday off," I lied.

Wednesday night I began the four-hour drive from Boston to New York. I don't recall what I did with my dog. I know I didn't bring her. I suppose I either dropped her off with my mother or left her in my apartment along with an apology and a pack of menthols. From a friend's apartment on the Upper West Side the next morning, I called work, explaining that my grandfather had been hospitalized. I wouldn't be able to make it in. I felt uncomfortable lying about my grandfather's health but told myself that he would be proud of me for getting a job in New York. Besides, for all I knew, he could have tripped and fallen that morning while trying to adjust his toupee.

"I'm not sure the Glenn Beck job is what I'm looking for," I told the CNN recruiter during our second meeting, a meeting that I had hastily arranged by saying that I had plans to be in New York again (another lie, another trip to the hospital for my grandfather). Perhaps she could find a few minutes for me, I had suggested. Our first meeting, a couple of weeks prior, had gone well enough, but it was kind of a blur, with her just trying to get a sense of my skill set. She had concluded with the dreaded "Let's stay in touch." That, of course, I knew, was code for "Larry King will be wiping his ass with your résumé before you hit the sidewalk."

I had to convince her that I was CNN material. "I saw on your Web site that *Anderson Cooper 360* has an opening for an associate producer. I'd love to be considered for that job." At the time, I wasn't too familiar with Anderson. I knew he had become a television superstar for his coverage of Hurricane Katrina, particularly the moment when he chased Senator Mary Landrieu down Bourbon Street and told her she was the Devil. Or something like that. I had no idea what kind of guy he would be to work for, if I even got the job, a long shot. All I knew for sure was that he anchored his own nightly show and America had fallen in love with his steely blue eyes, which were obviously tinted contact lenses.

"Well, that's a very competitive position," she said. "But I guess I could try to get you in for an interview. Let me call over there to see if the executive producers are around." The recruiter picked up the phone and dialed what I am convinced to this day was a fake number. After letting it "ring" for a bit she hung up and said they must be busy. So much for that, I thought. Maybe the CNN gift shop was hiring.

A gentleman should always stand when a lady enters the room. Especially during job interviews. I bounced to my feet and snapped to attention when Kathleen Friery, the executive producer of *Anderson Cooper 360°*, entered her corner office.

I'd been waiting for what I knew was a make-or-break moment in my career. At the exact moment she walked in, I noticed my fly was halfway down. If she saw me zipping up, she didn't let on, but I was convinced that in her mind I'd crossed over from "random applicant" to "random applicant who just finished masturbating."

I was as confident as one could be in an office overlooking Central Park, which is to say not very. I had Googled her before I arrived for the interview. People who say they don't Google a prospective boss are either liars or idiots. That said, I was so nervous, I was worried I would blurt out something that I had gleaned online. That I didn't respond to her statement of "Tell me a bit about yourself" by screaming "You went to Donald Trump's wedding?!" was a personal triumph.

Kathleen was Mary Tyler Moore, Murphy Brown, and Peter Jennings all rolled into one. Wickedly funny, gorgeous, with un-surpassed news judgment, she was everything I dreamed a big-time New York executive producer would be. She also had an extra set of shoes—expensive-looking ankle boots—underneath her desk. It was a sign of true power and importance, I decided, that one should require a mid-day change of footwear.

The interview must've gone well. A few days after I arrived home in Boston, I received a phone call from Kathleen offering me the job. I accepted on the spot. Either I was good or the only other applicant was a guy who actually was masturbating.

"Hi, I'm Jack, today's my first day," I said to Anderson Cooper the first time I saw him.

"I know who you are," he said, "I'm Anderson."

"Well, I know who *you* are," I said, shaking his hand like I was a politician asking for his vote. And then he disappeared into an elevator. The first week I worked at CNN, it didn't feel real. It felt like I was visiting and soon would be going home to Boston to resume my career in local news. There were so many new things to learn: production work flow, computer programs, vending-machine locations. I never missed an opportunity to remind someone that I was new, so that they would cut me slack when I fucked up—and I was going to fuck up. There was no doubt about that. It was difficult for me to adjust to the idea of working for one of the world's biggest news organizations. I was used to working at a place where I could get away with mis-spelling words like "governor."

That Anderson Cooper, though, he turned out to be a de-cent guy. Sure, he wasn't big on people making eye contact with him or staffers going into his office when he wasn't there, or even when he was there. But, that's not to say he didn't care. When it was your birthday or you did something worthy of praise, you would always get an e-mail from his assistant.

Anderson changed my life and career for the better in countless ways, and I'm privileged to call him a mentor and friend. And, really, how could I say anything bad about a guy who, years after I first met him by the CNN elevators, had the courage to have Kathy Griffin and me out to his country home on Long Island for a summer sleepover? It involved Kathy trying on Anderson's boxer shorts, me passing out on the sofa after too much sake with Kelly Ripa, and Anderson just sitting there, the whole weekend, giggling.

But stay out of his office if you know what's good for you.

I moved to New York in the middle of winter. The snow had a remarkable ability to silence the sounds of the city, just as the snowbank outside my building had a remarkable ability to silence the sound of the keys I dropped into it. I had started wandering around by foot, trying to get a feel for my new home. I'd already discovered that the only thing worse than a cabdriver who doesn't speak English was a cabdriver who does.

And, yes, there is the subway, but, frankly, you're better off missing the train than catching it, unless you like confined spaces and being sneezed on. So I did lots of walking. There were tourists, of course, and happy couples, too. I couldn't get around them fast enough. Every now and then I'd come across a couple dressed in matching morning exercise outfits. That's unacceptable before noon. Or, come to think of it, after noon. They're the same people who dress their Italian greyhounds alike or ask for more than one free sample at Pinkberry. Assholes.

For the first few weeks after I moved to New York, I felt nothing but excitement, though it didn't take long before I was exhausted. New York is beautiful and rich and full of adventure, but it's also fucking loud. On the plus side, I was able to get my antidepressants refilled anytime, day or night. I know other cities have those 24-hour pharmacies, too, but not on the ground floor of Matt Damon's building.

I began to spend my weekend days curled up in bed in my sublet. There was more than one Saturday afternoon when I wasn't sure if I was already in my pajamas for the evening ahead or still in them from the previous night. I sought solace in the comfortable and familiar, and by that I mean Bed, Bath

& Beyond, a store at which the shopping experience was so stimulating I needed a cigarette afterward. Occasionally, I went out to gay clubs alone, because I figured that's what a gay guy who didn't have any gay friends was supposed to do in New York City. For a while I was into dancing and fog machines. But I got scared off when a guy offered me crystal meth in a bathroom. At least I think it was a bathroom. Someone was definitely pooping.

My first roommate in New York was an attractive straight guy who, as far as roommates go, was pretty good, which means he didn't kill me. He did get drunk a lot. One night he came home bleeding from his face after an incident at an all-night deli. Because, you know, delis near Gramercy Park are known for violence. I tried to piece together the details of what happened; something about a price dispute and a broken door. Then there were the nights he didn't come home alone. We lived in a one-bedroom apartment that had been divided into two bedrooms, a common way of saving money in Manhattan. The only problem was that our wall was thin. So I could hear everything. And I do mean everything. Some nights I thought he was filming porn in there. Other nights the sex was so loud that I was just flat-out concerned about the structural integrity of the building. I mean, good heavens, young ladies of New York, where do you even learn phrases like that? I just turned up the volume of my *Golden Girls* DVDs.

I watched a lot of TV in that first apartment, and, for that matter, the second one, too. Both were sublet situations, which was nice because everything was already furnished and installed when I moved in. Then again, nothing felt like my own, as nothing was. The only time I felt at home in that first apartment was in the middle of the night after my roommate had gone to bed and I could watch TV alone in the living room. *Cheers* came on at 4 A.M., and *I Love Lucy* came on around sunrise. Maybe it was the sleep deprivation or maybe it was the occasional moan coming from my roommate's bedroom, but it became clear to me that the Ricardos and the Mertzes were only a few martinis away from going to a key party.

To this day I still can't get enough of those old reruns. If anything, my television viewing habits skew toward the elderly. Most of the shows I watch now—still late at night, still alone in my apartment—are filled with those life insurance commercials that remind us, in case we have forgotten in the past half-hour, that death is imminent. The setting is always a postfuneral brunch, and the ads center around two old ladies busy eating hors d'oeuvres and ignoring the dead guy's family. And if the commercials aren't about life insurance, they are about digestive problems and some wonderful new yogurt that solves them. Would someone give Jamie Lee Curtis a movie role so she can stop worrying about my bowel movements?

For most of that first year, apartment life in New York was similar—roommates and late-night TV—to apartment life in Boston. Except for the rent. In Boston I paid $600 to share the entire first floor of a house, complete with a yard and driveway. In New York my first sublet was $1,500 a month just for my portion alone. And my second sublet, well, that was a financial nightmare. It cost me $2,400 a month—which I could not afford then and cannot afford now. It was also a fifth-floor walk-up. Every night after work I had to climb all those stairs to change clothes for the dates I didn't have. But I was so naïve and uninformed about the Manhattan apartment market, and I was so desperate to find a place that accepted dogs, that I just gave up and took it. Thank God my roommate didn't ask for a security deposit because it took every dime I had just to pay the first month's rent. I was only there half a year, but it ruined me financially for the foreseeable future. I spent the next three years trying to dig out of major credit card debt. To save money I started buying shaving cream, spaghetti sauce, and underwear all in the same store. Hell, all in the same aisle. You don't realize how tight money is until you find yourself buying generic-brand lubricant. The hum of my air conditioner became remarkably similar to the sound of my electric bill not getting paid.

W ork life moved along. My new colleagues were nice, except the ones who weren't. But most were. Just beware of anyone who uses two emoticons in a row. A new job is like college. You never stay friends with the people you met that first year. Or maybe you do, I don't know. I hated college.

Occasionally a situation arose, but it's not like it was ever something that didn't occur in any number of professional settings. "I don't want to alarm anyone," a producer said, calling upstairs to the *Anderson Cooper 360* control room, "but I'm down in the green room and our next guest, well, I don't know how to say this, but our next guest looks just like Hitler." And he did, too. The guy looked just like Hitler. I don't recall his name or what he was there to discuss, other than it was something to do with counseling, which seemed doubly wrong.

After a year of sublets on the East Side, I realized I needed my own place. People suggested I move to Brooklyn. Cheaper rent and more space. Less stress, they say. But moving to Brooklyn means more time on the subway, where there is a fine line between overcrowding and unsolicited lap dances. And the added subway travel would take away from the time I spend on my sofa curled into a ball. No, thank you, Brooklyn.

My new place ended up being a tiny studio in the West Village. It's cliché, but I had been in walk-in closets bigger than that apartment. But it was my own place in one of the city's most desirable neighborhoods and a "bargain" at $1,750 a month. After experiencing two sublets that were at best lukewarm about dogs, it was crucial for me to find a place where my Labrador retriever, Sammy, and I would be welcome. The brokers assured me that the building allowed dogs so, naturally, when I moved in with Sammy, the super came up to me and said, "We don't allow dogs." Luckily, he didn't seem to care beyond that, but that didn't stop me from living in fear of eviction for the next ninety days. Apparently there's some law in New York City that as long as your landlord knows what you're up to for three months, you can keep on doing it after that, even if it's not in your lease. I was pretty sure my upstairs neighbors had a mechanical bull.

The apartment was on the first floor. Initially I had trouble sleeping because of the noise from the drunks outside the corner bar. I considered taking Ambien, but was scared off by my friend Lisa's experience with it. She would pop a couple of pills and call me at 1 A.M., under the influence, ranting about Tupperware and coffee creamer. But I got used to the noise, and in time grew to love the West Village. I was not in Kansas anymore, at least according to the guy dressed like Judy Garland urinating on Christopher Street late one postironic Halloween. Even though I was living there decades after its heyday, the neighborhood was livelier than anywhere I'd ever called home. It was being invaded by heterosexual yuppies offering all-cash deals on bland condos, but the piano bars were still there, as were the occasional drag queens on Seventh Avenue. Closer to the Hudson River, there was what my grandmother—if she hung around gay leather bars—would call a "slightly rougher" crowd. And in between there were the shops and townhouses and intellectual-looking pedestrians that gave the Village its real estate charm. I even found a therapist I liked in the neighborhood, who would stop mid-session to show me his acting reel on YouTube. It turned out that in addition to being a therapist he was also a professional TV and movie extra. What? Your therapist wasn't on *Boardwalk Empire*? Our sessions usually began with "So, how's your depression going?" I'd reply, "Great, I'm sleeping so much I haven't had time to think about it." That never seemed to be the answer he was looking for.

The only downsides to the West Village were the tourists and the rats. The tourists were easy enough. No matter their nationality or what they asked me, I always replied, "Bob Dylan's old apartment is that way," in French.

But the rats, they terrified me. I'm pretty sure some of them were responsible for muggings, possibly knocking over a few convenience stores. They darted out of nowhere, and some of them were bold little fuckers, staring you down until you backed up and reversed direction. More than once I rerouted myself down better-lit streets because I'd come to know where the rat gangs hung out. I'd heard that the excessive rodent population was because of all the old buildings in the neighborhood. The nooks and crannies of centuries-old townhouses apparently gave them spots to live, breed, and hide. Frankly, I think it was more of a waste-management issue. Hardly an evening goes by in Manhattan that you don't have to dodge garbage bags on the sidewalk. And on the rare occasion you don't, you're dodging and weaving drunk couples pawing at each other. One way or the other, it's always trash night in New York City.

The daylight, however, belonged not to the rats, but to the rest of us. And once the cold weather started to lift that first spring, it was magic on the West Side of town. You could smell it in the air, that blend of tree blossoms and unpaid rent. And, naturally, everyone said, "Spring has sprung," which is a phrase I don't like. Not just because it's hackneyed but also because it sounds like the tagline of some seasonal Viagra ad campaign. Once I was watching television with Chet Curtis and a Viagra ad came on. After the disclaimer "If you experience an erection lasting longer than four hours, call your doctor," he shouted, "Hell, if I have an erection lasting longer than four hours, I'm going to call everyone I know."

Spring always sneaks up on me. It takes me a bit of time to shift from my cranky, rushing-around-the-city-trying-to-get-inside-from-the-bitter-cold mode to a more leisurely frame of mind. Many New Yorkers welcome the warmer weather because it gives them the chance to showcase their toned bodies. I am not one of them.

It's almost pointless to walk over to the Hudson River Park with any sense of self-esteem. Everyone talks about how New York is filled with good-looking people. I brushed that off for my first year or so. But, once I started going over to the river . . . it was like a scene from a movie, a movie that could get dirty in a hurry. Beautiful people show a lot of skin. And the closer to the Hudson River they get, the more skin they show. I planned to take my dog with me on my first day hanging out there, so I would at least have some sort of lame excuse to strike up a conversation with these exquisite creatures. Unfortunately, the New York City Parks Department doesn't allow dogs on the grass there. Smoke as many joints and get into as many loud couple fights as you want, but don't bring your dog. And, of course, the only open spot on the grass was not next to glistening Brazilian exhibitionists rubbing cocoa butter on each other, but a couple of miserable yuppies. "Evan, I *told* you to pack my Fiji water," the woman said. The guy just sat there, beaten down, in madras shorts looking out onto the water, presumably pondering the new life he could start for himself in New Jersey if only he knew how to swim.

My apartment in the West Village was so small that I had to purchase a loft bed frame from IKEA to have any real living space, however diminutive. I can't assemble anything, but my friend Mark is handy with tools and will work for beer. So, one Saturday I tossed can after can of Coors Light at him until he got the bed frame set up. "Bed frame" is a bit of a misnomer. It was so rickety and unstable, it was more like a metal hammock on stilts.

A year later, thanks to Mark's handiwork and my lack of a sex life, the setup was still intact. I was lying in bed around 12:30 A.M. doing what I normally do (no, not that), watching *Golden Girls* clips on YouTube, when I got an e-mail from my boss. "You up? Plane crash. May need you to come back in," she wrote. I started to get ready. Confirmation that I needed to be back uptown came moments later.

I said goodbye to Sammy, ran out of my apartment, and hailed a cab. "Columbus Circle," I said, "as fast as you can."

"Did you hear about the plane crash?" I asked my cabdriver. He hadn't. As we sped up Eighth Avenue, I dialed into the network-wide conference call that goes into effect during breaking news. Reports from the scene in Buffalo indicated everyone on board and one person on the ground had died. Fifty souls.

Anderson was there by the time I got to CNN. At that point, because of the late hour, coverage was being remotely produced from our Atlanta headquarters with help from our upstate affiliates. We made final preparations for Anderson to take over anchor duties from New York. The network was mobilizing staff and resources, but we didn't have a full crew on hand at the Time Warner Center. We could, however, go live by using a camera position in our newsroom that required no on-site crew. Our colleagues in Atlanta could control everything robotically until New York was staffed. Unfortunately, it became clear that there was a problem with the camera. Atlanta couldn't control it. I stepped behind the large machine and attempted to move it toward the position where Anderson was hooked up to the microphone cord. The thing wouldn't budge. I looked like a maniac, wrestling with this camera—which was beyond expensive, God help me if I broke it. We stayed on the air until 4 A.M. when we handed off to the *American Morning* team. It was a long night, a sad night.

That's the worst part of working in TV news—it's sad. Every day there's tragedy, more tragedy than one can understand, let alone put on the air. Anderson, as everyone knows, has been all over the world and covered many awful, heartbreaking events. I don't go with him on those trips, I have colleagues much more experienced and talented who produce that level of reporting. I don't know how they do it. I'm much more comfortable covering the stories that don't come with tragedy. I'd rather stay in the newsroom and crack jokes, making fun of politicians, teasing colleagues, even teasing Anderson. Viewers know by now that he has a terrific silly side, when he's not yelling at staffers or kicking puppies. I'm kidding, of course. He doesn't yell at staffers.

I got lucky not taking that Glenn Beck job. I'd like to think I'm smart enough that I wouldn't have ended up on his crazy train. But not only was I young, I was impressionable and timid. Hell, it was six months before I had the nerve to stand up to Anderson and refuse to feed his parakeet.

Some days I still can't believe where I ended up working. To quote Anderson Cooper, "Anderson Cooper is a big deal." Though, it's not as glamorous as most people think. Nothing ever is. First of all, he hogs the helicopter. Second of all, the man has shown zero interest in picking up my dry cleaning. He is generous in other ways, though. He's made some celebrity connections on my behalf. And let me just say, regardless of whether I was—as I believe—on Sandra Bullock's yacht or—as the police report states—in my hotel room clutching a bottle of cough syrup and watching *Speed* 2, I regret those late-night phone calls to Wolf Blitzer.

I should mention, every year Anderson does invite the staff to a barbecue at his country home, though he makes us do yard work before we can eat.

Still, he's a hell of a guy, that Anderson Cooper. He ended up being terrific to work for. I owe him a debt of gratitude that I will never be able to repay.

But the blue eyes—totally fake.

WENDY FOR PRESIDENT

Democratic National Convention—Denver, Colorado—August 25–28, 2008

Republican National Convention—Minneapolis/St. Paul, Minnesota—September 1–4, 2008

I awoke in Minneapolis with two realizations: my hotel pillow smelled like dog food, and Regis Philbin was referring to himself in the third person. I had no reason to believe there was a connection, but one can never be sure. Years later I would see Regis in person as he delivered a "speech" at a Friars Club event honoring Larry King. I then would understand that talking about himself in the third person was the least of his problems.

As I flipped through the channels, I saw that Sarah Palin had done a walk-through of the Xcel Center in advance of her highly anticipated speech that night. Palin looked poised, if a bit apprehensive, though no one could fault her for that. Republicans had their fingers crossed that she would establish herself as the Alaskan Margaret Thatcher. Democrats were hoping she'd come across as a woman whose biggest gubernatorial accomplishment was enforcing igloo zoning laws.

Everyone was buzzing about Palin's attractiveness, a shallow line of political commentary. There would be no such conversation, people argued, if she were a man . . . or, it later turned out, if the RNC hadn't given her $150,000 for a new wardrobe. Her old clothes were most likely still covered in blood from the previous Christmas, when she blew Rudolph's head off.

I was less fixated on Palin than I was on the stage the Republicans had set up. It looked like something from a Liza Minnelli surplus sale. The only conclusion I could draw from the glistening black laminate was that there must be a cabaret portion of the convention. I began looking forward to John McCain singing "Baby, It's Cold Outside" with Nancy Reagan.

I suppose I shouldn't have faulted the Republicans for trying to ratchet up their glamour quotient. There was no way they could have beaten the Democrats when it came to celebrity attendees, so why not incorporate stagecraft to complement Newt Gingrich's jowls?

For its part, the DNC was so full of movie stars that they blurred together. In theory—like any good low-level cable news producer, desperate to feel relevant—I should have loved it. But in reality I was exhausted and cranky. Instead of indulging my fetish of writing *Thelma & Louise* quotes on scented stationery and slipping them underneath Susan Sarandon's hotel room door, I bitched about my boss, Anderson Cooper, who stopped to talk to Rebecca Romijn-Stamos on our way out of the convention grounds. I know, I know . . . she divorced John Stamos so that's not her name anymore. But that wasn't the worst part. The worst part was that it *wasn't* Rebecca Romijn-Stamos. It was that it would serve as a VIP lounge, a place where power brokers could unwind and—after a few drinks—appear on CNN. Staffers of my ilk weren't allowed to eat there—a policy I found unacceptable. I hadn't traveled halfway across the country to be denied my God-given right to make sweet, sweet love to a CNN-subsidized milkshake. Eventually, I would get hold of a VIP pass that provided me entry, but in the meantime I was limited to the work space when I wanted a breather, figuratively and literally.

One afternoon Anderson and I noticed then CNN anchor John Roberts (the poor man's chief justice) taking hits from a little container of compressed oxygen. Apparently it wasn't such an unusual sight in Denver, the Mile High City. Even though we weren't having issues with the thin air, we asked John to share, and for the next few minutes we amused ourselves by huffing down squirts of oxygen and seeing how long we could hold our breaths. We didn't feel much of an effect but we were definitely onto something: politics would be much more bearable if everyone were doing whip-its.

Compared to most journalists covering the convention, I had it pretty good. And it would be hypocritical of me to complain given how much I enjoyed the whole experience. It was a glorious chaos that dovetailed politics and show business. Not to mention the perks of traveling with Anderson. "No, no, no, this will simply not do," I clucked at the Denver rental car center upon learning the CNN Travel Department had reserved me a compact vehicle. "Look," I said, leaning over the counter, "I'm going to be driving around a *very* important person. Ralph Lauren Black Label was not made to be worn in a Chevy Cobalt, whatever that is. I want a luxury car. I'll settle for an SUV. But not just any SUV, I want the kind you rent to rappers embroiled

Charlize Theron—something I realized just as I was abou
open with my icebreaker, "So, does your husband stay in t
with Candace Cameron?"

Speaking of Susan Sarandon, I was displeased to see h
my post-DNC flight home to New York. That's one downsi
living in New York. There is always a celebrity on your f
which quickly goes from novel to annoying. Because if
going to hit a flock of birds and crash-land in the Hudson
the last thing I want to have to worry about is Susan Sara
stealing my limelight on the rescue boat and reducing my
ism to a blurb buried in between Dear Abby and a massag
lor coupon.

But to be fair to the celebrities—because that's wha
portant—they were not the only ones who slowed us do
we moved around the convention sites. The delegates
selves caused major delays for our team, clambering for a
of Anderson. And I'm talking about both sides of the p
aisle. Seriously, if you're looking for true bipartisanshi
need look no further than Anderson Cooper fans. Ever
we went, people wanting photos and autographs mobbe
Being the nice guy that he is, he obliged, but since I'm
who'd get fired if he didn't make it to the set on time, it
to me to say "no more." I tried to wave people away, tellir
that Wolf Blitzer was down the hall letting the Florida
tion braid his beard.

We learned that our only places of refuge from the
were the CNN work spaces—large rooms filled with c
laptops and troughs of granola bars. In Denver our wo
was above the CNN Grill, a restaurant the network ha
adjacent to the convention center. The idea for the

in gang wars." I left, grudgingly, with a Ford Explorer, but made up for it the following week when I arrived in Minneapolis for the Republican convention. I pulled out of the airport in a white Cadillac that would have made Boss Hogg jealous. There's nothing like driving a car that costs more than you make in a year to make you feel simultaneously giddy and despondent.

It's only in hindsight that I wonder what I was thinking. How I ever got that expense report past the CNN accountants is beyond me. I assume it had something to do with the manner in which I emblazoned Anderson's name in every section labeled "Business Purpose." Transportation for Anderson Cooper. Dry cleaning for Anderson Cooper. Chicken nuggets for Anderson Cooper. "Oh, you didn't know?" I would deadpan if questioned on my expenditures, "Anderson can't go a day without a McRib."

In many ways the conventions that year were milestones, the last of the truly enjoyable moments in a campaign that seemed like it would last forever. This should have been over long ago, I thought to myself. I knew it was a bad sign when my analysis of the election started to match up with my analysis of Paris Hilton's fame. Burnout was inevitable, I suppose.

The criticism of the national conventions is that they're essentially free television infomercials for the candidates, which is true. All possibility of intraparty conflict is eliminated days, if not weeks, beforehand. Even the prime-time portions end up being rather dull save for the occasional Clint Eastwood sideshow. That said, I don't know what—in this era of staying on message at all costs—would qualify as compelling political programming. Even the general-election debates later that fall had me longing for something more enjoyable. Perhaps that night in college when someone put out a cigarette in my hair. As Senators Obama and McCain debated, I thought of my friend Lisa. Lisa taught me that life should be viewed through the lens of Old Yeller, the ill-fated dog from that gut-wrenching Disney movie. She turned Old Yeller into a verb. At least once a week Lisa and I text each other, "Please Old Yeller me." After five minutes watching those debates Old Yeller would have turned to his master and said, "Alright, just take me out behind the shed and let's get this over with."

To an extent, I was surprised that I'd developed such a cynical attitude about our electoral process. I was a political nerd as a kid, memorizing the names of all the presidents in chronological order. And although it was a skill I was proud of, it did not impress my classmates. My talent underwhelmed even my own father, who felt that I should spend less time on government trivia and more time outside playing sports. In those days the possibility of my ever having any connection to a presidential election, let alone covering it for CNN, would have been beyond comprehension. I'd been to the 2004 DNC, so I had an idea of the kind of dog-and-pony show the Democrats had in store. And although I had never been to an RNC, I had produced my then local station's 2004 election night coverage from Bush headquarters in Washington. Talk about a surreal night. I remember someone telling me early in the evening that it was "Kerry in a landslide." After that, everything was a haze. For weeks I had a nightmare where I was missing a shoe and playing Texas Hold'em with Condoleezza Rice on the floor of the Dulles Airport Cinnabon.

Of the two conventions in 2008, the DNC was arguably the more exciting place to be. Never mind the crowd's palpable enthusiasm for the nominee, the Democrats had an unbeatable lineup of political superstars: Michelle Obama, Bill and Hillary Clinton, and an ailing Senator Ted Kennedy—a guaranteed showstopper if there ever was one. What the RNC had that the DNC didn't—besides many more white heterosexuals—was my colleague Brittany Harris. Poor Brittany. After a long day at the convention site, all she wanted to do was unwind in her room, call her fiancé, and alphabetize her complimentary hotel bath products. But, uncomfortable being lame and socially awkward by myself, I kept knocking on her door, dangling the keys to my rented Cadillac like a pimp in ill-fitting pajama pants.

Most of the time we just ended up aimlessly driving around Minneapolis in a futile attempt to come across an A-list event or at least run into Sam Donaldson and his hair. On the final night of the convention we returned to the hotel in our brothel-on-wheels, greeted by the bright lights of the nearby Wendy's, the only remaining nightlife option. As we walked across the street to indulge in an order or ten of fries, I figured we'd hit rock bottom. But I was wrong. Rock bottom isn't going to Wendy's because you have nothing better to do. Rock bottom is going to Wendy's because you have nothing to do and discovering that the door to the restaurant is locked. I did not take it well.

Before I could find a brick to throw through the door, Brittany noticed that the drive-thru window was still open. We were on foot, but I didn't think that would be a problem. There were no cars around. I suppose I was naïve in thinking anything, even fast food, could be that simple.

First, we tried to order at the squawk-box menu board, but there must have been a weight sensor in the drive-thru lane that we weren't heavy enough to trigger. That was frustrating at the time, though, in hindsight, it was probably a good thing. My self-esteem was low enough without being mistaken for a minivan.

Stymied at the squawk box, we advanced to the pickup window. You would have thought we were wearing ski masks and armed with AK-47s. The worker inside Wendy's freaked out, waving us away and shouting through the glass something about security. Confused, I tried to explain that we weren't there to rob him. We only wanted Biggie Fries. Judging by how far his eyes were bugged out, my statement came through on the other side of the glass as, "We're robbing you *and* we want Biggie Fries." My luck didn't change after telling him I was Senator McCain.

It was only after he shouted, "Cars only!" that Brittany and I realized what was going on. Walk-ups, we later learned, aren't allowed at Wendy's drive-thrus, at least not that one. If we wanted those French fries—and oh, Sweet Mother of Sodium, we wanted them—we'd have to come through in our vehicle. So back we walked to the hotel, returning about ten seconds later in the tugboat-sized Cadillac. "Helloooo, it's us again," I singsonged into the squawk box. I figured if the guy thought we were armed robbers, we should at least be polite. He took our order and we pulled forward to the pickup window, eager to enjoy our last supper in Minneapolis. This time the attendant was all smiles. He explained to us that there had been reports of thieves operating on foot. Pedestrians at drive-thrus, it seems, like politicians at conventions, need to be viewed with a healthy dose of skepticism. We apologized for the misunderstanding, expressed concern for his safety, and then, of course, robbed him.

IF LOVING SHOULDER PADS IS WRONG, I DON'T WANT TO BE RIGHT

I don't know why my grandparents sleep in separate bedrooms. Maybe it's generational. Maybe it's, as my grandmother once said, because my grandfather tosses and turns too much. Or, maybe they're each having affairs.

Unconfirmed octogenarian adultery aside, I have more in common with my grandmother when it comes to sleeping habits. She's fond of naps during the daytime and stays up late into the morning, reading romance novels and watching low-budget murder mysteries. At least that's what she says she's doing. I wouldn't be surprised if she had a vicious online poker habit. And, of course, in her salad days she wasn't above falling asleep with a lit cigarette in her mouth.

My grandfather wakes up before dawn, barreling through the day until he calls it a night at 4 P.M. If he wakes up in the middle of the night, he is likely to watch a hockey game, or listen to the sounds of invading foreigners. He knows they're coming.

When we were little and my sister, Rose, and I would sleep over at our grandparents' house, Grammie would take the living room sofa so Rose could have her room and Bumpy would sleep on an Army cot in the basement so I could have his. Blind to their hospitality, I couldn't say goodnight to them fast enough, breathless to experience the multitude of cable channels at my disposal, by which of course I mean the nonstop parade of simulated sex known as Cinemax.

Grammie and Bumpy lived a half-mile away, if that, from our house. Still, those overnights seemed so exotic, they might as well have been a week in Tahiti, not that I knew where that was. That my grandparents had cable was a suburban siren song. And even though they didn't know how to use it, they had a VCR *with a remote control!* It was like taking a tour of NASA, except with lots of snacks. That was their strategy, I think. Whereas my other grandparents, the Greeks, would bring out the board games and insist on a big loud meal for everyone, Grammie and Bumpy—true to their WASP roots—would toss us some Carr's water crackers, make small talk for about twenty minutes, and then dispatch us to our respective television sets. It's not that they didn't enjoy spending time with us, it's just that WASPs don't like to risk board games. Someone could slip up and show an emotion.

Saturday-night sleepovers were the best. Even when I was little, I could tell that it was the most exciting night of the week. If my parents were only going out for the evening, they would just get a babysitter to come over. There was one who reported that my first word was "Reagan," a clever attempt to get more money from my Republican father. I remember the smell of my mother's perfume as she got ready. To me, she was a movie star; a movie star who encouraged me to pass the time by watching the dance program *Solid Gold*. She knew even then that I was a sucker for anything with a theme song performed by Dionne Warwick.

But on the Saturday nights when my parents went out of town, they would drop Rose and me off down the street at Grammie and Bumpy's house. Jackpot. Saturday nights in the 1980s and early 1990s meant one thing: *The Golden Girls*. The theme song, the wicker furniture, senior citizen libidos, I couldn't get enough of it then and I can't get enough of it now. I don't know what it was that got me hooked. I suppose at the time it seemed naughty and dangerous—something I shouldn't be watching at an impressionable age. One time, annoyed at my sister for taking one of my toys, I called her a slut. Loudly. In front of my entire family. She was six years old. "But," I protested, "I heard Dorothy say that to Blanche last weekend." That defense was unsuccessful.

I'm not sure if my parents knew, when they took us to Disney World in Orlando one year, that the exterior set of *The Golden Girls* was part of the MGM Studios back lot tour, but I didn't. And it's a good thing, too. I would never have been able to sleep until we got there. For most nine-year-olds in those days, the highlight of a trip to Disney World was Space Mountain or Typhoon Lagoon, or perhaps, for the science-minded, Epcot Center. Not me. My mother had to restrain me from jumping off the trolley once I realized I was looking at the home of my four favorite shoulder-pad aficionados. I don't know what I intended to do when I got up to the house. I'm sure I would have somehow tried to chain myself to it. Or maybe I would have licked the garage door. Alas, I never made it out of the trolley. The driver kept right on going, past the house from *Empty Nest,* past the house from *Encino Man,* past the house from *Ernest Saves Christmas,* none of which I gave a shit about. All I wanted was to break into that beige ranch and fall asleep to the sounds of Bea Arthur singing "Mr. Sandman."

There was something so adult about the experience of watching that show. Sitting in my grandfather's den, which reeked of pipe tobacco, with Oliver the gastrointestinally objectionable beagle at my feet, watching these naughty old ladies talk about S-E-X, I felt like a rebel. Granted, I didn't get most of the jokes. The episode in which the ladies buy condoms left me particularly confused. But I knew the show was for me. It was funny, it was cozy, it had heart. It was everything I wanted for my life, I just didn't know it yet.

And then one day the sleepovers stopped. I don't remember when. I just remember that one day I was old enough to stay home alone. Suddenly, spending time at Grammie and Bumpy's house on Saturday nights didn't seem so exciting. I would drive past their place as I tried to make it home before curfew. Some nights the lights in their bedrooms were on, some nights they were off. No more grandchildren sleeping over. All was quiet, aside from Oliver's occasional farts.

And then one day I was in college. I had my own place. I was no longer tiptoeing down to my grandmother's kitchen to get more Orange Milanos during the commercial break of the episode when Blanche thinks she's pregnant. And, let's be honest, if any of those girls was going to get pregnant, it was going to be Blanche.

It was at my studio apartment in New Hampshire during my sophomore year of college when I became reacquainted with Dorothy, Rose, Blanche, and Sophia. Sitting on the carpeted floor, flipping through the channels of the television, eating a bag of peanut butter cups—an unfortunate dietary habit I've still not been able to kick—I heard the familiar "Thank You for Being a Friend" theme song playing on Lifetime. It was like wrapping myself in an old blanket and inhaling deeply. A tingle went up my leg. I'm not saying that when I saw the opening credits I got an erection. I'm just saying there might have been some movement in the area.

Lifetime was branded as Television for Women. Maybe it was, but it was also Television for Jack, whether they wanted me or not. I was back in, hooked on the pastels and cheesecake of post-menopausal Miami dames. I could not have been happier. It was the fall of 1999 and the presidential campaign was in full swing in New Hampshire. Back-to-back episodes of *The Golden Girls* were the perfect way to offset days and nights spent obsessively following a political cycle that, although compared to 2012 seems tame, was grueling. I remembered my grandmother saying to me once that she liked how hotels always offered *USA Today* because, no matter where she was, she felt like she was at home. I felt the same way about *The Golden Girls*. And I think we can all agree that *that* is the hallmark of a well-adjusted college guy.

Watching *The Golden Girls* as a nineteen-year-old was a different experience, and not just because I understood all the sexual references (except the one about stirrups). I realized it was progressive and compassionate, values to which I hadn't given a lot of thought at that point in my life. It wasn't as if I became an overnight activist, preaching the book of Rose, Dorothy, Blanche, and Sophia. Sure, I went around quoting them, but that was more of an effort to make friends at the campus smoothie bar than anything else. It was more of a subconscious effect, informing my worldview on life's lessons: we all will get old, AIDS doesn't discriminate, divorce is something to keep a sense of humor about, there's nothing wrong with being gay, friends and family are worth fighting for and crying over. And, of course, it's not cheating if the guy's wife doesn't find out.

Years went by. I changed apartments. I changed TV sets. Which is more than I can say for Lifetime. They knew a good thing when they had it, and they doubled down on those *Golden Girls* reruns, airing them in the mornings and in the evenings, with the occasional weekend marathon. Wherever I lived, I always knew Lifetime's channel number. In those years before I acknowledged to myself I was gay, my television viewing habits presented a dilemma. As an ostensibly straight guy, how was I to explain my love of a show that revolved around four women and their costume jewelry? Well, I didn't. I kept my *Golden Girls* time to myself, especially during the years I had roommates and avoided advertising my addiction.

It was only after I moved to New York and started to come out that I could embrace my love of the show. I had friends from college and Boston who knew, but they were few and far between. In New York I could answer the question of "What are you doing tonight?" honestly with "I'm going home to watch *The Golden Girls* and cry." Oh, come on. Like I was the *only* person to tear up when Rose's boyfriend has to leave her to enter the Witness Protection Program. The episode ends with her quoting Robert Frost. They don't make TV shows like that anymore.

I know this doesn't make any sense, but I insist that I was the first of my friends to discover text messaging. I swear that I was the one who realized we had this odd feature on our phones, years before it exploded. But, someone else can take credit for that. I don't care. What I will not let anyone else take credit for—at least no one my age—is for "rediscovering" the American treasure known as Betty White. I was a devoted fan years before *Saturday Night Live* or TV Land got in the Betty White business. I was quoting Rose Nylund to my cat Rusty a solid two decades before Ms. White rocketed back to much-deserved TV stardom with her lifetime achievement speech at the Screen Actors Guild Awards. Not that I wasn't thrilled by the attention she received in 2010. I loved that in an entertainment culture dominated by Kardashians there was still room for someone with talent.

Like any job, working in television has its own kind of monotony. Even the opportunities to meet celebrities become a bit unremarkable after a while. Still, that doesn't mean that I wasn't eager to meet Betty White. She was my last chance to make an in-the-flesh connection to *The Golden Girls*. By 2010 all the other cast members had passed away. I had never gotten to meet Bea Arthur. By the time I moved to New York, she had stopped performing on Broadway. I always dreamed that one day we would get together for lunch and gossip and then maybe do some kickboxing. Sadly, Estelle Getty battled dementia for years. I never got to quiz her about her wig or why she didn't get an Oscar nomination for playing Sylvester Stallone's mother

in *Stop or My Mom Will Shoot*. And I so regretted not hauling my
fat ass out of bed to make it to Rue McClanahan's book signing,
missing my chance to ask her to record my outgoing voicemail
message to go with my *Golden Girls* theme song ringtone.

So when I heard in June 2010 that Betty White would be—
gasp—in the CNN building to tape an appearance on Joy Behar's talk show, I knew my chance had arrived. A friend of mine,
who worked on the Behar show and had tipped me off to the
visit, encouraged me to hang out by the studio to ask Ms. White
for a photograph. I was so nervous. It was like the episode when
the four roommates are all waiting for President Bush to stop his
motorcade at their house for a photo opportunity. Their plotlines were so realistic.

I started to see staffers running around. Some I recognized,
others I didn't. All of them were giving me dirty looks. I pre-
tended to be typing on my BlackBerry. One even snarked to
my friend, "Why do you have the paparazzi waiting for her?"
Because it's Betty Fucking White, that's why. Just be glad I'm
wearing pants. Voices were hushed, the air was fraught with
tension. "Betty is on a tight schedule, they're taking her right
into the studio," someone said. I had a bad feeling. The pudgy
homosexual with the cellphone camera will not be meeting
America's Sweetheart. Well, I don't know what kind of polyester
pantsuit delivery truck they thought I'd just fallen off, but I was
not going to be deterred.

I went back to my desk, turned on the in-house feed, and
watched the taping. When I sensed it was wrapping up, I ran
down a back hallway to the studio door, barreling through like
the platonic life partner I knew Betty White had always wanted
me to be. I stayed up against the wall, trying to be invisible, my

head craned to see if she was coming my way. And just like that, there she was.

Like an elderly angel sent from above, she stepped toward me, followed by an entourage larger than ones I'd seen accompanying heads of state. Swarmed by members of Joy's staff and crew, she obliged by posing for photograph after photograph. Her handlers started saying "last one, last one." That was my cue. I pushed through the mosh pit until I was right in front of her. I extended my hand and said, "It is an honor to meet you, you've meant so much to me over the years." And at that crucial moment, the moment I'd dreamed of, Betty White was everything I'd hoped she'd be. She looked me right in the eyes, gave me a warm smile, and said, "Oh, thank you, that's so sweet, I'm so glad to meet *you*." And then, with her handlers glaring off to the side, I got my photo, which I e-mailed to everyone I knew and uploaded as my Twitter profile picture. I may have also told people that we were engaged and registered at Macy's.

For people in their eighties, my grandparents are fairly tech-savvy. They know how to check my Twitter page, they know how to use e-mail, and, of course, "The Google." But even though they read my tweets and saw me once on CNN talking about how great Betty White is, I'm not sure they understand why I'm such a fan. It's not like when I stayed over at their house as a kid we began breakfast by discussing which estrogen-driven sitcoms I'd watched the night before. So when I e-mailed them the picture of her and me, they thought it was cute, but I don't think they dwelled on it. If they thought I was having sex with Betty White, they didn't let on.

I suppose if I saw them more often, perhaps I'd find the time to explain to them how it was less about Betty White and more about them, how watching reruns of *The Golden Girls* transports me back to those days when everything was warm and cozy, and not just on Cinemax. But we're WASPS and we don't delve much into feelings. We stick with what we've always done best, a few minutes of small talk before they go to their separate bedrooms.

THE CAMERA ADDS 27 POUNDS

His name was Scott. He had a perfect smile, ridiculous biceps, and was a former Abercrombie & Fitch model. I hated him.

Scott was my "personal trainer"—a phrase I enjoyed throwing around until I got my American Express bill. He worked at the New York gym where I had a membership—Equinox, which apparently is Latin for overpriced. I would show up each morning, hoping that he had gotten a call from Susan Lucci to give up his fitness career to play her cabana boy, Pierre, thus sparing me the torture of his workouts. In hindsight, I was an idiot. Not only could I ill afford Scott's services, it was as much an exercise in vanity as physical fitness. I was playing right into the cultural cliché: an insecure Manhattanite spending hours working out, desperate to get his body fat down to a level that would let him score a mediocre hand job in the alley behind the Times Square Red Lobster. (Hey, you have your clichés, I have mine.)

At the time, I was still new to the city and CNN. I thought I was comfortable with who I was, but it turns out one's self-esteem takes a heavy toll when faced daily with the movie star good looks of Anderson Cooper and James Carville. Plus, everyone in Manhattan is thin. It's not that there aren't fat people. There are. They're called tourists.

It wasn't that I was exercising only to be more attractive on the outside. I welcomed good health. While I'd never been a fanatic about blood pressure and cholesterol, I soon became unyielding in my devotion to a proper cardio workout . . . unless there was a compelling reason to stay home, like it was cloudy outside or I was watching *The View*. On the positive side, I had long since quit smoking and was making a good-faith attempt to curtail my love affair with chicken fingers. Though I was reticent about living in a world without breaded poultry.

My diet has never been conventional. I don't like pizza. To this day I have never tried bacon. I've also never eaten a bagel. And I don't care what you say, I refuse to believe I'm the only person who has his generic store-brand mayonnaise shipped to New York from Massachusetts. So please don't try to make this about me. I'm the sane one here. I'm the one who knew he hated gnocchi without even tasting it. That "gn" consonant pairing, that "nyo" sound, I am *all set* with that scene, thank you. I'm just an old-fashioned believer in the four food groups: grains, dairy, Twizzlers, and black-market muscle relaxants. So take your gotcha politics somewhere else.

I'm surprised I could afford any food, with the money I was paying Scott to watch me do squats. At the time, my membership dues and personal-training sessions seemed like funds well spent. I was healthier, I had more energy, and—unless I looked at myself naked—I felt good about my body. Unfortunately, there was something I didn't yet realize about New York City gyms: Even the best ones end up being where self-esteem goes to die. Just when you think you're starting to get results, you wind up on a treadmill behind a twenty-two-year-old with a body as tight as a snare drum. Cue the quiet sobbing in the stairwell.

When I lived in the West Village, I worked out at a gym filled with beautiful people. At least that was an incentive to keep doing crunches. But then I moved uptown and the median age of my fellow gym-goers jumped to ninety-seven. Downtown, I worked out next to actresses I would see later in the week being interviewed on the *Today* show. Uptown I worked out next to senior citizens I would see later in the week being wished happy birthday on the *Today* show. The only thing worse than watching an old lady exercise while a curtain of flesh dangles from her arm is the realization that she can bench press more than you.

When conventional workouts left me frustrated, I decided to try yoga. Yoga is for people who are Zen or have a foot fetish. I don't fall into either category, not even after a few drinks. And there's something disheartening about being there in my hideous sweatpants, stained with crumbs of cheddar Goldfish crackers, unable to touch my toes, while the woman next to me, who just gave birth that morning, wraps her ankle around her neck. I wish I liked yoga. It seems so healthy and intelligent. Turns out my favorite pose in yoga class is called Leaving Yoga Class.

Like any good hypocrite working in television news, I have—despite my expensive daily exercise routine—pitched the occasional segment on unrealistic body images. "Magazine ads, couture models, movie stars . . . they're ruining society," I argue, because blaming Madison Avenue and Hollywood for the tribulations of the world is so original and newsworthy. "Beauty is on the inside," I lecture to anyone who will listen, which is no one. And then I go to the gym.

It's a tough sell, the beauty-is-on-the-inside bit. We say it not because we believe it. We say it because we think it makes us sound like kind and decent people. "Looks don't matter to me, it's all about personality," someone will say. I'm impressed by anyone who can say that with a straight face. And I'm still waiting for the study that shows average-looking people with good personalities have lots of sex. The truth is, we don't. And if we did, I wouldn't have time to read the study because I'd be too busy having orgasms.

My other favorite argument about appearance is, "Beautiful people are just like the rest of us. In fact, most of them are plagued by insecurity." No. What most of them are plagued by are fame, fortune, and sexual options so numerous that they need to ice their loins after scrolling through their missed calls.

Sure, there's always the exception. I once had dinner with a popular film actress with whom I have a mutual friend. It would be indiscreet for me to reveal her name, so let's just say it rhymes with Jessica Biel. This actress was and is absolutely stunning—gorgeous, truly. And, as one apparently does when dining out with a movie star, we went to an upscale Manhattan restaurant. I'd been there before alone and, of course, couldn't even get my water glass refilled. This time we were seated in some special VIP booth that I didn't even know existed.

It was ridiculous. And yet, this actress—whose name rhymes with Jessica Biel—was delightful. She was sweet, generous, unpretentious—everything I wanted in an attractive celebrity dining companion who'd likely already forgotten my name. But the best moment was when I mentioned how great the French fries were. Her eyes lit up as she said, "Ooh, let's get two orders." Granted, that was probably just because she didn't want me touching her food but, still, I embraced it as one of those *Us Weekly* "Stars, they're just like us!" moments. Finally, I thought to myself, a member of the glitterati—other than Kirstie Alley—who shares my passion for trans fats.

When the food arrived, she ate only one fry (with her fork) while I stuffed fistfuls into my mouth. But by then it didn't matter, the illusion had been shattered. She had started talking about her boyfriend—whom I'll just call Justin Timberlake—and I was reminded that stars are definitely not like us.

It's not just movie stars whose bodies blow my mind. The comparatively low-rent world of cable news is filled with good-looking people who would run over their grandmother to get to Pilates class. Network executives love to tout the diversity of their on-air staff. But make no mistake, diversity means African-American, Latino, Arab, and Asian. It does not mean overweight. I say that like I'm in favor of going to Times Square and rounding up a bunch of chubby women sporting home perms and fanny packs and putting them on television. Absolutely not. If I wanted to watch the day's top stories reported by someone with a bloated face and discount rack jeans, I'd videotape myself.

It's brutal, but true. The few times I've done on-air work have been enough to jolt me into a crash diet. They say the camera adds 10 pounds but from my experience it clocks in right around 27. We have great makeup artists at CNN, but they're not miracle workers. I walk into the makeup room and they're like "Whoah, I didn't sign up for this shit." They spray-paint my face with an air gun and say things like "I'll try to make it look like you have cheekbones." And now that most of our cameras are high-definition, watch out. I ended up looking like the love child of Tyne Daly and Abe Vigoda. And that is not a look America wants.

We turn on the TV or go to the movies to see attractive people. People we lust after, people we fantasize about. Perky blondes who all look the same and who may or may not know anything about journalism, sultry brunettes who may or may not know how to act . . . let's not get mired in job qualifications. Guys, take off your shirts; ladies, whip out a boob. That's the American way.

Now that I am personal-trainer-less, the burden of staying in fighting shape rests on my shoulders. Many days I fail. Occasionally, I haul my fat ass onto the elliptical machine and watch TV as I attempt to burn off the peanut cups I ate on the way to the gym. I find myself distracted by the multiple television sets. I'm not sure if I'm more aroused by *Days of Our Lives* or the commercial for Dairy Queen. Exercising is painful, and I may never have Justin Timberlake's pecs, but I'm no longer doing it for my career. Just a bit more time on this earth. Or at least a bit more sex.

Besides, the chicken fingers never loved me back.

MY NEW ROOMMATE KEEPS LICKING HERSELF

I've never met a Labradoodle who wasn't an asshole. I don't know what it is about that particular breed, a cross between a Labrador retriever and a standard poodle. At least I think it's a standard poodle. Perhaps I've just never seen a miniature poodle humping the back end of a chocolate lab. Either way, they're insane. I remember the first Labradoodle my dog Sammy and I ever encountered. He was bouncy and curly-haired and, I assume, he answered to the name Hannibal Lecter. Every time we passed this dog, he would try to murder Sammy. The dog's owner would never stop him. The most I ever heard him do was mutter an apology and burp, as he continued on to the Art Garfunkel look-alike contest.

As obnoxious as it was, at least that dog was on a leash, which is more than I can say for the amorous fellow at the dog park who used to approach Sammy with the canine equivalent of a snifter of cognac and a Barry White album. There's nothing quite like starting your day by watching a four-legged arthritis sufferer named Harvey try to fornicate. A Folgers Crystals commercial from hell.

I once made the mistake of sharing my thoughts on Labradoodles with one Mr. Anderson Cooper. Next thing I know he was telling our then news anchor Erica Hill that I basically had a collection of them stuffed and mounted over my mantel. So allow me to set the record straight: I don't have a "pathological disdain" for Labradoodles, as Mr. Cooper would have you believe. All I'm saying is that, as far as I can tell, "hypoallergenic" actually means "pistol-wielding thug."

All dogs have their flaws. Sammy is far from perfect. She licks my pillow. She licks my sheets. She gets excited when I take down the bottle of Malibu rum that I keep next to her box of biscuits on top of the refrigerator. She's a rascal and, I suspect, a bit of a drunk.

Like any responsible adult who cares about animals, I brought Sammy into my life on impulse, with no forethought. It was 2004 and I was living in an apartment in Boston. I probably should have reviewed the terms of my apartment lease, which stated in unequivocal bold print that pets were not allowed. But there I was, in the midst of one of my semifrequent bouts of depression, when it hit me: "I know what will cheer me up. A puppy!" To those of you who are going to argue that clinical depression isn't a good reason to get a dog, well, I don't know what animal experts you've been talking to. All I know, it was either buy a dog or take my pills, and I was out of pills.

I turned to the classified section of the newspaper and

thumbed through the Pets for Sale advertisements. OK, OK, stop your badgering. First I went to the pet shop. There, are you happy now? I know, I know, pet shops are awful. They buy from puppy mills. They charge astronomical prices. But I just looked, I didn't purchase. Instead, I soon found myself driving up to Maine in response to an ad by a breeder for Labrador retriever puppies. Well, "breeder" might be a strong word. It was a lady in a house on a dirt road whose dog had given birth to a litter. I'm not sure if there were tears in her eyes or dollar signs, but the puppies were damn cute.

On my way there I told myself I wasn't necessarily going to get one, but I stopped at the bank just in case. I was a bit excited and maybe talking a tad rapidly. I told the teller how I was withdrawing $400 to go buy a puppy. I think she interpreted that as code for some sort of amphetamine. Walking into the "breeder's" house—which looked like the house from *The Brady Bunch* if the Bradys were antigovernment survivalists and Alice was selling stolen DVD players out of the laundry room—that uniquely puppy smell hit me. It's basically cuteness mixed with urine.

There must have been ten of them, all black except for a yellow one. They rushed toward me like a hurricane of adorableness. If being swarmed by a puppy pack isn't one of life's great joys, I don't know what is. About thirty seconds after my arrival, the question wasn't if I was going home with a puppy but which one. The "breeder" told me that she was keeping the yellow lab, but the black ones were available. Fur racist. I've read that homeless black dogs are less likely to be adopted because some people perceive them to be scary. Idiots. A black puppy was more than fine with me. But I still had to select which one. I asked the lady if there were any females, since the dog I grew up with was a female. What can I say? I love my bitches. Fortunately, there was only one female available. My choice was easy. I held her up to my face and looked into her wide, scared puppy eyes. I was in love. But I felt guilty, too. How could I rip this poor little creature away from her mother and brothers? Intellectually, I knew that's how things worked for domesticated canines. All I could do was vow to love her and care for her always . . . as long as she didn't scratch up my hardwood floors.

The ride home was nerve-racking. I had put Sammy—even though she wasn't Sammy at that point; she was like one of those poor infants whose yuppie parents can't decide whether to name their baby after a grandparent or after their local Brookstone—in the front passenger seat. She didn't move an inch for thirty minutes, staring directly into the seatback. I was worried she was hurt, until I stopped at my mother's house and realized that the puppy's quiet, focused demeanor was not because she was injured but because she'd spent the past thirty minutes peeing into the upholstery.

My mother was excited to meet the dog, almost as happy as she was seeing me take a break from being depressed. We tried coming up with a name. At one point my mom walked in from the other room, where she had been watching the news. "What about Laci?" she asked. "Hmm, that's not that bad. . . . Wait a minute, Mom, were you just watching a story about the Laci Peterson murder trial? Is *that* where you came up with that name?" We kept thinking.

After a few hours visiting my mom, it was time to head back to my apartment in Boston and introduce Sammy to her new home. I made a mental note to call my roommate. I'm a considerate person and nothing says considerate like letting the person you live with know that you've purchased a nonreturnable puppy. But I had to stop on the way and show off my new best friend to my dad and my grandparents, all of whom are huge dog-lovers who go to bed before sunset.

I called ahead at seven-thirty to announce that I was stopping by with someone new in my life, someone whom I'd like them to all gather together to meet right away. I couldn't help but fuck with them. "You're really going to like *her*," I said. "She's going to be just crazy about you." It was too easy. Pulling into the driveway with Sammy, who by now was traveling in a plastic laundry basket, I could see the lights on inside the house. I picked up my furry bundle of joy and headed down the walkway to the side door where my father was waiting for me. He burst out laughing. As we walked into the kitchen, I saw that my grandmother had put *caviar* on the table and a bottle of *champagne* on ice. As if I were coming over on a random Monday night to announce my engagement to someone they'd never met. Had she confused me with one of my cousins? My dad hollered upstairs to my grandparents. They came downstairs in what I can only describe as mothball evening wear. It was as if they'd not only gotten dressed in a hurry, but had done so drunk with the lights off. As soon as he saw the puppy in my arms, my grandfather rushed over to me so fast, I thought his toupee would fly off. When I left an hour later, he summed it up, "This is much better than any girl you could have brought over." Talk about a topic for another day.

Back in Boston, I took Sammy upstairs to the apartment, a steep third-floor walk-up, something else I probably should have considered in addition to my building's ban on dogs. My roommate T.J. was smitten right away. He told me he knew it was going to be a lot of work, a lot of late nights and early mornings, but he said he couldn't wait to help take care of her. And then he left to spend the night at his girlfriend's house.

That first night I woke up in a cold sweat. I was panicking. What had I done? I had just committed to spending the next ten to fifteen years with this poor little creature. Friends said to me, "Why didn't you just get a cat? They're so much easier." I like cats, but they don't really love you like a dog. Though, if I ever do get a cat I'm going to name her Stevie Nicks and make her wear a cape. It's the right thing to do.

Sammy and I made it through the first week. By then her name was Sammy, after a series of aborted choices. I ran into strangers at Petco who would fawn all over her and then ask me her name. More than once I got the response, "Sammy?! What kind of name is that for a girl dog?" Fine, it's short for fucking Samantha, if that makes you feel better, OK? Now how about you and your rigid gender norms go back to the fish food aisle where you belong.

There were also people who made it clear that they did not like dogs. "I'm not a dog person," they said. Those people confused me. When someone says, "I'm just not a dog person," I have no idea what that really means. Just say, "I'm an asshole," it's quicker.

I learned a lot those first few weeks. The most important lesson was don't turn around to attend to your puppy in the backseat while stopped at a red light, because you will take your foot off the brake and hit the car in front of you. Oops. Also, don't spend too much time texting at the dog park, because your dog is probably knocking small children over. And when you show up at the animal hospital emergency room for the third time in two days, wearing boxer shorts and a rain poncho you got for free, screaming, "My puppy is dying, my puppy is dying," the staff might begin to ignore you.

Back then I didn't put a lot of stock in experts of any kind. That was long before I realized it's David Gergen's world, we're just living in it. But I started to read up on proper dog care. Everyone seemed to be in agreement: you must crate your puppy. "Crate," of course, is a cozy little word for cage. I don't know how many focus groups it took for the pet care industry to come up with "crate," but it's a cage. That said, I couldn't get Sammy into one fast enough. I slammed that door behind her like she was the last inmate into Alcatraz. I put her in there when I went to work, and I put her in there at night. She was not happy. When I left for work, I would stand outside my apartment door and wait to hear if she cried, which she always did. I started leaving the television on for her during the day. Even a lonely puppy can't resist a Maury Povich paternity test episode.

Sammy couldn't bear not sleeping in my room at night, but the TV was in the living room, so I would have to lug the crate out there every day when I went to work. Back and forth, back and forth. The damn thing wasn't light. And every time the landlord came around, I had to scramble to hide everything. My life was an *I Love Lucy* episode. Unfortunately, the building wasn't owned by Fred Mertz, or even one of those management companies from whom you at least know what to expect and when to expect it. It was some mom-and-pop operation. The guy would show up randomly, with no given warning. Sometimes he'd stick around for five minutes, sometimes for two hours. It was not ideal, especially when I needed the landlord to come into the apartment to address a maintenance issue or, I don't know, *a massive rodent infestation*. If you've never had a mice problem, take my word for it, it's a special kind of terror. Walking into your own bedroom—drunk—and flipping on the light to see a dozen tails scurrying into the corners is not a welcome home. The mice army grew so strong that they exiled Sammy and me to the living room. I called an exterminator but he said I'd have to get written permission from the landlord before any work could be done. And I knew if I called the landlord he'd want to come into the apartment and poke around. What was I supposed to say? "You can't go into my bedroom. Pay no attention to the whimpering. I know it sounds like a puppy, but it's just my roommate with a ball gag in his mouth."

At least the mice didn't bother Sammy in her crate. Which is more than I can say for visitors to my apartment. One night, when I was entertaining a lady friend—back when I still entertained lady friends—Sammy was sound asleep in her crate when my overnight guest had to get up and use the bathroom. Everything was fine until she tripped and fell over the puppy's crate. Naked.

It wasn't long before I let Sammy out of the crate to sleep on my bed. Just for one night, I told myself. Then two nights passed, then three. That was it for the crate. Once you wake up to a puppy with her head on the pillow next to you, staring at you with those wide eyes, there's no turning back. Within the span of a week, my bed became her bed, my pillows became her pillows. The experts warn you not to let your dog become the leader of the pack. I don't know if she was technically the leader of the pack, but there were definitely nights when I tried to get her to move over and she would give me the finger.

Eventually we settled into a routine. I would feed Sammy, walk her, and provide her with the best care that my maxed-out credit card could buy. In turn she would climb on my head while I was eating and refuse to walk down the stairs. One morning I was carrying her down the three flights and I missed a step, plummeting on my back to the bottom of the staircase. I guess some sort of protective instinct kicked in because I managed to hold on to her. When the dust—or mold or whatever the hell was in that death trap—settled, we both paused a beat and looked at each other. Then, just as I was about to burst into tears from the pain, at the moment I needed a kiss the most, she gave me a big lick across the face and a look that said, "That was fun, can we go again?"

Years went by. I got out of that apartment, I got a new job, and I left Boston. I experienced great success and great disappointment, excitement, and heartache, but, thankfully, no more mice. The only consistent part of my daily life—aside from anxiety and a store-brand multivitamin—has been Sammy. I can hardly believe she is eight years old. The expressive and mischievous eyes are still there, but now so are the signs of age: a bit of white fur along her chin, a slower pace to her walk. I can't imagine her love of food will ever abate, nor her love of belly rubs or hatred of squirrels. But time is not kind to man's best friend. I've been down that sad road before. I can't even bear to think about it.

There's nothing like having a dog. Even, I suppose, a Labradoodle.

DECK THE HALLS WITH BOUGHS OF XANAX

JetBlue, always messing with my head. In the summer of 2010 the airline had a promotion whereby travelers could purchase unlimited fares within a one-month period for a flat rate of $599. What a deal. Perfect for close-knit, cash-strapped families; families who had been, until then, forced to choose between visiting grandma at the Home and attending cousin Luther's intervention. I did not take advantage of the offer as I had prior plans to be shot out of a cannon.

Don't get me wrong. I love my family. It's just that the idea of traveling home with any frequency is, well . . . "nauseating" is such a strong word. As much as I'd like to make exceptions for the holidays throughout the year, I don't. When I first started working in TV, I used to love visiting with my relatives. I had an interesting—even glamorous—job and people bombarded me with questions. It was nice to feel smart and successful. But, in the past few years I've not made it home that often, not even for Thanksgiving—an admittedly selfish choice. I regret it. The enormous spread of food, football on the television, family members exploring the fine line between alcoholism and narcolepsy—America at its finest.

Officially, I tell my family that, despite the holiday, I have to work. Which is true, give or take eight hours. When pressed on my absence, I remind my parents that we once ate Wendy's takeout for Easter. So, as far as I'm concerned, if God can overlook us swapping out the body of Christ for Frosties, surely my Aunt Vicki won't mind if I skip her annual feast of turkey and passive aggression.

Invariably, my phone rings on Thanksgiving morning. It's my mother, wishing me a happy holiday. She says she understands that I couldn't make it home, a hollow sentiment belied by a voice filled with melancholy and Mimosa. Over time, I've learned that the way to assuage my mother's seasonal empty-nest syndrome is to convince her that my Thanksgiving in New York is anything but dull and lonely. I do what any good son would during such a phone call: I fake my attendance at the Macy's parade. "Hi, Mom. Happy Thanksgiving to you, too. Yup, I'm watching the floats go by on Central Park West. Look to the lower left of the Garfield balloon. I'm wearing a red hat. Do you see me? I'm waving. Do you see me? No, a *red* hat." And then I go back to my Cocoa Krispies and DVR'd erotica.

Truth be told, my mother, Maria, is my biggest champion, the person who is most proud of my career in New York. She visits me regularly and has been to CNN for a tour. And while she has never been one to embarrass me, I was nevertheless anxious ahead of her meeting Anderson. I knew she'd want a picture with him. No problem there. It was what else she might want that concerned me. I mean, my mother is as polite as they come. That doesn't mean she's above surreptitiously smelling Anderson's hair or asking him to autograph her knockoff Gloria Vanderbilt jeans.

Fortunately, Mom's visit to CNN ended up being low-maintenance. Which is more than I can say for some distant relatives who have showed up at the Time Warner Center. It's always a treat when people take me up on my "offer" of a tour, apparently thinking I was serious. I thought everyone realized "If you're ever in New York, stop by my office, I'd love to show you around" is code for "Go away, your lazy eye is creeping me out."

Being a child of divorce, and thank God for that, I have two families to manage. Grammie and Bumpy are my dad's parents. In New England, Bumpy is a nickname for grandfather whereas in New York it's more likely a stage name for a drag queen. Grammie has been the de facto ruler of the family since Bumpy's mother, Nana, passed away. A death which, by the way, had nothing to do with the time I knocked her off the front steps and into the shrubbery. If Nana were alive today, she'd tell you that the azaleas broke her fall. Frankly, she had it coming.

As for Grammie, she's one of those lifelong New Englanders who seem like they came out of a Hollywood casting office. Her ancestors go all the way back to the Mayflower era, or so she used to tell me as she clipped her toenails. They were the ones at that first Thanksgiving in Plymouth saying, "That's a beautiful centerpiece, but where's the bar?" In many respects Grammie is the archetypal grandmother. A former teacher, she loves cooking, gardening, and knitting. Not to mention her other maternal interests like grandchildren and Benson & Hedges 100s. When I was a child, and she wasn't smoking cigarettes the size of yard-sticks, Grammie would make me strawberry milkshakes and regale me with stories of her early years. Most of those stories involved her one-eyed pug, Tiny Tim, whom she would push around in a baby stroller.

These days during our visits, I tell the stories while Grammie does the listening. The topics rarely vary: life in New York, major political stories, and which celebrities have visible panty lines in real life. And now, instead of a milkshake, I'm offered a glass of wine. As it turns out, Grammie is no slouch in the adult beverage department. Lest one get the wrong idea, know that my grandmother—while never one to decline a cocktail, especially on a holiday ("Well, we have to do *something* for Flag Day Eve")—is a woman of elegance and restraint. She steadfastly adheres to the No Drinking Before Five O'Clock rule, she just sets her clock ahead six hours. But, what's the big deal? All she has is a vodka martini or four—no different than any other God-fearing, stroke-surviving, pacemaker implantee. Not that the rest of the family should concern themselves with her health, we're reminded. When Grammie was rushed to the hospital after suffering a stroke, we were told by my father that she "just went to the doctor's for some tests." When she dies, I expect to hear from him, "She's in the hospital but don't worry, her condition has stabilized."

Even though I've skipped Thanksgiving for years, Christmas is slightly different. The slight difference being that my grandparents hand out cash. Coincidentally, it's the one holiday for which I show up. When the time comes on Christmas Day for the family to eat, Grammie sits at one end of the table, with Bumpy at the other. Always the last to take her seat, she strolls in—as everyone waits to dig into their prime rib—with her plate full of lobster. Yes, lobster. Just in case we forgot who can piss the farthest. Menu inequalities notwithstanding, the meal itself is always a delight, especially the moment several years ago when Grammie, in between bites of foie gras, used the word "whore." Apparently when she's not doing shots of blood thinner, my grandmother channels *The Real Housewives of New Jersey*. I can't really complain, though. She treats me like a prince, never failing to remind everyone at the table that I work for CNN. Or, as she puts it, "Channel 42—the one with that guy we don't like."

As I crush up a horse tranquilizer into my mashed potatoes, I look around the table for any sign that I'm not at a reunion of extras from *One Flew Over the Cuckoo's Nest*. There's my cousin Zachary, a firefighter who hasn't spoken since the Reagan administration. There's his brother, Willie, whose girlfriend opened his eyes to the exciting world of cat ownership. Then there's my father, a man whom I am committed to one day put in a nursing home against his will. Dad's specialty was signing me up for sports teams behind my back. There was soccer, which I objected to on the grounds that there wasn't a snack bar. There was basketball, which discriminated against those of us unnerved by buzzers. He also signed me up for baseball and football. He said they built character. So do nursing homes, Dad.

At least when Nana was alive, you could count on her for some amusing dinner-table guilt trips. I was too young to realize it at the time, but Nana was a devout Swedish evangelical and thus the family's resident party pooper. She objected to a range of things: cigarettes, rock 'n' roll, Catholics. Nana also didn't like that no one came to visit her. I was too scared to tell her that no one came to visit her because even on the rare occasion someone did, all she talked about was how no one came to visit her. If only I'd started smoking pot at a younger age, Nana would have been a lot more fun, as she spent most of her day eating Vienna Fingers and watching bowling.

On Christmas I'd be enlisted to go with Bumpy to pick Nana up from her assisted living complex. "Hey, big boy, it's time to go pick up my motha," he'd say in his thick Boston accent. We would pull up to her building in his Chrysler New Yorker, which sent the old ladies scrambling like the Beatles had just landed at JFK Airport. They'd rush over, thinking it was their family coming to pick them up for the holiday. I felt so bad, I wanted to pile them all in. "Sorry, girls," Bumpy would say, as we guided Nana and her walker to the car. The drive was only ten minutes, but that was plenty of time for Nana to lodge an array of grievances. Usually they had to do with some distant relative whom Bumpy had forgot to wish a happy birthday. And she always found time to retell the story of how twenty years before she had been robbed by an "Oriental man." My sister says our family isn't particularly unusual. I remind her she spent her first eight years out of college working as a therapist for drug addicts and dementia patients.

As for Bumpy, well, what can you say about a man who buys his toupees in packs of three? He is outgoing and loyal without fail. A fountain of encouragement, he always told me that my career dreams—much like his pouch of discount pipe tobacco—were within reach. He didn't have any contacts in the TV news industry, a fact he lamented more than once. But he helped me in other ways. Most notably, he gave me a car. It was a baby blue 1987 Chevy Celebrity wagon, but still. As with most milestones—especially his changeover from a black hairpiece to a white one—my grandfather had impeccable timing, giving me the car at the height of my high school insecurity. Nothing makes a seventeen-year-old more self-confident than a battered station wagon from the previous decade.

To my surprise, even though I would have preferred something red and Italian, the Celeb—as my friends and I called it—would come to serve me well. It was clean, the engine started on cold mornings, and the brakes—unless I needed to stop—worked great. I took it to college with me, and in the summer of 2000, I drove it three times a week from southern New Hampshire to suburban Boston for my internship at WCVB-TV, the region's ABC affiliate. It was during that summer that my directional lights malfunctioned. I had to blink them manually by moving the lever on the steering column up and down whenever I needed to turn. If you ever want to feel like a misfit, I suggest manually blinking your Chevy Celebrity directional light as you enter a TV station parking lot behind a line of BMWs.

Bumpy is aging. He is walking slower. He says "Just promise if I start to drool you'll pull the plug" more frequently. He kicks off the discussion at his end of the dinner table by reminding everyone where he wants his ashes spread. You know it's time for dessert when he gets to the part about salvaging his gold fillings.

But Christmas is no less festive. He still presides over the living room as our own personal Santa Claus, albeit one demoted from handing out gifts. His method of squinting at a tag, hollering "I can't read this fucking thing," and then flinging the gift toward the fireplace led Grammie to decide that he was better suited to collecting the used wrapping paper. He sits teetering on a folding chair trying to catch the balls of crumpled-up paper that are being thrown at his head, muttering, "You sons a bitches."

I used to give Bumpy consumables for Christmas, like candy or cookies or, his favorite, Cracker Jacks. But then one year he thanked me by saying, "Jesus Christ, are you trying to kill me? Didn't I tell you about my diverticulitis?" so I switched to John le Carré novels. No matter which one I give him, he's already read it. Most people ooh and ahh when they open presents. Bumpy takes one look at something and shouts, "Christ, I hope you saved the receipt." The only gift he ever likes is the one he gives himself. Each year it's the same thing, a pair of orthopedic wingtips that appear to be made entirely out of rubber. Bumpy has long favored shoes that can be hosed down in the yard.

After dinner—which, because we so enjoy each other's company, takes about seven minutes—everyone moves back to the living room. Bumpy announces he has finally quit smoking and then excuses himself to go outside, where we notice him smoking his pipe. Then he does that thing that old men with pipes do. They walk around with their hands clasped behind their back, inspecting their yard while wearing a baseball cap emblazoned with the insignia of an aircraft carrier. Sometimes I join him for one of these walks, eager to share one of life's tender holiday moments. A tender holiday moment, it turns out, is Bumpy listing the reasons why he'll never buy a car made in Japan.

After his smoke, Bumpy comes back into the house to spread more holiday cheer. He shows everyone the BB gun he uses to scare off the squirrels that loiter around his bird feeder. It's quite a comforting sight: an eighty-one-year-old man, carrying a rifle and wearing black wraparound sunglasses that he got after his cataract surgery.

The wine runs out. It's time to go. Bags are packed, cars are warmed up. But before everyone leaves, Bumpy stands up to make an announcement. "Hey, hey, hey," he says, getting everyone's attention. "In all seriousness, I want to thank you all for coming"—and then, pausing a beat—"because I probably won't be around next year."

W hen I was a kid, both sets of grandparents lived within a short distance of each other. It was a great way to see all your relatives on a holiday, if you're into that sort of thing. After celebrating with my dad's side of the family, we'd head to my mom's side. Christmas with the Greeks is like Christmas with the WASPs, only hairier. The celebration was usually held at one of my aunts' houses. My mom is one of four sisters and at any given time at least two of them aren't speaking to each other. There are always two of them in the kitchen trashing the two in the living room. It's a Christmas tradition.

My Yiayia is far from the stereotype of a loud, boorish Mediterranean grandma. She is sophisticated and stylish. Which means she wears pearls when she's choking the life out of a lamb with her bare hands. A humble woman, Yiayia implores her children and grandchildren to eschew any semblance of extravagance. And no, you're not allowed to bring up her nose job and Cadillac.

Yiayia is married to Papou. Papou looks like Michael

Dukakis. If Dukakis had been elected president in 1988, my grandfather could have had a lucrative side gig as his body double. A renowned doctor who instilled in me the importance of hard work, honesty, and—when he wasn't looking—complimentary Vicodin from his office, Papou is now a hermit. From what I can tell, he spends his time in the basement eating Walmart-brand peanut butter cups. Occasionally he'll leave the house, either to get more peanut butter cups or to explore a local cemetery. CNN would get much better ratings, he explains as he shows me a hand-drawn graveyard map, if we'd just do more stories on dead people.

The highlight of Christmas with the Greeks is the Yankee Swap. A northeast tradition, it involves putting cheap gifts into a pile and picking numbers out of a hat. If you want to know more about it, Google "holiday fisticuffs." The Yankee Swap gifts are traditionally divided into three categories: wine, lottery tickets, and expired ibuprofen/surplus catheters, which I'm pretty sure is the same kind of stuff that Mary and Joseph were hoarding in the manger. As the items are chosen and people start to swap, it's not uncommon to hear such holiday pleasantries as "Get away from me, you bitch" and "Why don't you show everyone your new tattoo, skank." And that's just my grandmother.

Christmas with the Greeks never lasts as long as Christmas with the WASPs, in part because it's later in the day, and in part because everyone's wasted. But the truth, on both sides of my family, is that the holiday magic—if that ever really was a thing—is gone. Everyone is grown up. Divorces and remarriages have dotted the years. Sometimes everyone shows up, sometimes everyone is scattered. The years when my generation got excited about unwrapping presents, the years when our parents were still young, are over. We tuck away our Christmas checks that we will use to pay off credit card bills and college loans. We check to see if our flights are on schedule the next morning.

Christmas Day isn't officially over until Papou chases our car down the driveway and tries to give us a twenty-dollar bill for gas. Twenty dollars doesn't go as far as it used to, and neither does Papou. But I like the tradition.

Maybe next year I'll buy that JetBlue pass.

MY LIFE IN DOGS

Sammy didn't come into my life until I was twenty-four. At that point I'd been without a dog for about nine years, since my childhood dog, Whitey, died. Whitey was black. She had a prominent patch of white on her chest and some white around her paws, but she was a black dog. A mutt, some sort of lab mix. My father named her. He always claimed he chose the name because of her shock of white fur, but the name always embarrassed me. It didn't make any sense. Why was my black dog named Whitey? As I got older, I began to wonder if my poor dog was politically incorrect. But by then I had so many other issues with my father that I was too exhausted to play the canine race card.

Whitey and I were the same age. My parents got her as a puppy when I was about a year old. As family legend goes, they previously had a dog named Pepper, who tried to eat me. My dad took Pepper to the local animal shelter, where the staff promised to find her a good home. After leaving, he had second thoughts and returned twenty minutes later. Pepper, of course, was already dead. Or, as my grandfather so delicately put it over the years, "Pepper got the needle." I just love that my dad was about to give hungry Pepper a second chance with his infant son. One of many facts I've filed away for a rainy day of elder care planning.

But Whitey never tried to eat me. That's not to say I'm convinced she liked me, or the rest of the family for that matter. She was always trying to escape. She knew how to open both the front and back screen doors. My parents installed a six-foot-high fence in the backyard, which kept her contained for about a day and a half until she saw one of the cats jump over it and followed suit.

And, yes, we had cats. Over the years we had six of them. Toni, Valene (named after a character on *Knots Landing*), Rusty, Sandy, Greenleaf, and Phantom. The only cat that liked me was Toni. The others were too busy killing moles or drinking antifreeze in the neighbor's driveway (RIP, Greenleaf) to give two shits about me. But Toni was sweet and liked to be held. Before I was born, my mother would dress her up in baby clothes and carry her around the house. She lived to an insanely old age, like seventeen or something. At the end she had one tooth, like a purring calico meth-head.

The cats taught Whitey how to escape the backyard fence, and escape she did, repeatedly. And it wasn't like she strolled around the neighborhood. She got the fuck out of there. Once she bolted into a neighbor's garage, poked her head into some grocery bags, and helped herself to a pound of sirloin. Another time she hauled ass down to the main road and promptly got hit by a car. My grandfather—of "All Dogs Go to Heaven After They Get the Needle" fame—took special care to tell me that Whitey's leg was hanging on by a thread. Poor Whitey. But she recovered.

We had only one sofa in the living room. Referred to as "Whitey's sofa," it was disgusting to the point of crusty. Out of a 24-hour day, Whitey probably spent 23 hours and 45 minutes on that sofa. When my mom tried to donate it to the Salvation Army, they refused to take it. Whitey rarely ventured into other rooms of the house, certainly not mine. Once, after I watched the movie version of *Annie* for the three hundredth time, still trying to perfect my choreography of "You're Never Fully Dressed Without a Smile," I decided that Whitey and I would be best friends like Annie and her dog, Sandy. Unfortunately, Whitey had no interest in me, or whether I ever made it out of Miss Hannigan's orphanage. I tried to get her to make my bedroom her favorite spot in the house, but she clawed at the door like she was a Saint Bernard digging someone out of an avalanche. It's a nice boost for a boy's self-esteem when even his dog doesn't want to hang out with him.

Grammie and Bumpy lived down the street and always had a beagle, which from my experience is a good breed for crazy WASPs. Often they want a pet that will make them seem comparatively normal. When I was a small child, they had a beagle named Bosley. He was just average beagle size, but at the time I thought he was a horse. My father had gotten Bosley as a puppy a decade earlier to live at his college fraternity house. That living arrangement lasted a week. Then one day he had to be put to sleep—Bosley, not my father—which was my first brush with the death of an animal. I was young enough, though, that the grown-ups kept it away from me. Not long after, my sister and I went with Grammie and Bumpy to the pet store to meet a potential new member of the family.

My grandparents had spotted a beagle puppy in the window, and they wanted to see if he would be well behaved with us, as we were at their house nearly every day. It turned out that the little guy was a lunatic, but if you've ever seen a beagle puppy, you know that it doesn't take long for one to win you over. My grandparents brought him home and named him Oliver after— wait for it, because this is a good one—Colonel Oliver North. At the time he was embroiled in the Iran-Contra scandal. That was their idea of a good namesake. And I'm related to these people. By blood.

Oliver fit right in at my grandparents' house. Within his first month he ate a piano leg and a third of a Barcalounger. That was before he got thrown out of obedience class. He was also a howler. Friends, relatives, the mailman especially—Oliver announced everyone's arrival with such cries that you would have thought his balls, if he still had them, were attached to a car battery.

But he was a good and loyal dog. Every morning he, my grandfather, and my grandfather's toupee would walk to the center of town to buy the newspaper. In the winter he would snore next to the radiator on the fancy L.L.Bean bed my grandmother bought him. In the summer he would seek relief from the heat by curling up next to the base of the toilet. Don't get me wrong, Oliver was mentally ill and spent the better part of a decade and a half vomiting up pieces of furniture, but never once was he anything but gentle and loving with my sister and me.

My other grandparents, Yiayia and Papou, weren't into beagles, but they loved German shepherds. They had two named Zorba and Sparta, just in case anyone couldn't tell from Papou's eyebrows that he was Greek. But that pair was before my time. I grew up with their shepherd Abby. Stable and stern, possibly a loan shark, Abby was the opposite of Oliver and Whitey. She had no interest in running away or destroying the house. All she wanted was to be near my grandparents. My grandfather loved to take her with him for a ride to the town dump in his pickup truck. Rugged and manly, except he was a doctor who lived on a lake. Nice try.

When we kids—my sister, cousins, and I—were at the house and playing on the beach, trying to drown each other and getting fishing lures caught in the trees, Abby's herding instincts kicked in. She would be on duty, patrolling the perimeter, making sure none of us left her line of sight. And then at night, after a long day of swimming and fishing, when we were all inside, doors locked, watching TV in the den, she would walk into the room, lie down on the carpet, and let out a huge sigh, her work done for the day.

Years later Abby got cranky. She started taking down local kids who had the nerve to bicycle past the house. She never hurt any of them, but because communities don't like when their bicycling youngsters are ambushed by a 100-pound German shepherd, Abby spent most of her golden years confined to a porch or inside with my grandmother watching Sally Jessy Raphael.

Everyone knows not to mention Abby to my grandparents. Many years have passed, but Yiayia and Papou still cry over her. She was their last dog.

My dad called me at college the night Oliver was put to sleep. He said that Bumpy had teared up, which in WASP-speak is code for meltdown. Several months later I broached the idea of getting another puppy to my grandparents, but they were done.

Whitey's long life came to an end during my parents' divorce, a period of tremendous trauma and chaos. She collapsed one day when I wasn't home. I never saw her again.

Sammy is now a canine senior citizen. She walks a bit slower and sleeps more. I recently switched her food over from "adult" to "mature adult." They say it makes for a longer, healthier life. It's probably just a marketing scam, but I'll give it a try. I need her to live forever.

THE (LARRY) KING AND I

The first time I saw Larry King in person was the summer of 2004. I was working on-site at the Democratic National Convention in Boston. At that point in my career, it was the most exciting assignment I'd ever had. The place was crawling with journalism legends, political icons, and Hollywood stars. Hillary Clinton, Bono, Barbara Walters, Puff Daddy, they were all there. My head was on a swivel.

In a hallway inside the FleetCenter, I squeezed past a little-known state senator from Illinois who smelled like cigarettes and was there to deliver the convention's keynote address. No entourage, just him and another guy. When I got back to our workstation, I rattled off to my coworkers a list of the celebrities I had seen. "Oh," I added as an underwhelming afterthought, "I also saw that guy from Illinois, the one who's giving the keynote.

What's his name again?" A colleague, looking at a piece of paper, said, "Obama . . . Barack Obama."

As far as TV news stars, there was none more iconic than Larry King. I first spotted him one day as I ate dinner at Dunkin' Donuts on the ground floor of the FleetCenter. He appeared out of nowhere, headed toward an escalator. I was breathless. Trim and spry, he made his way through the crowd before the slack-jawed onlookers could react. It was all over in seconds. I barely had time to wipe the chocolate sprinkles from my mouth, much less go up to him and say hello. Larry was gone, up to his sky-box to hang out with anyone who was anyone. Anyone but me.

As luck—and blueprints of the building—would have it, I ran into Larry later in the week when I happened by the CNN work space. "Mr. King," I said/screamed as I calmly approached/chased him down the hallway and extended my hand/placed him in a headlock, "may I have a photo?" Ever the class act, he agreed, though he drew the line when I asked to try on his suspenders.

It was a moment for which I had been waiting my whole life, or at least since my grandparents got cable. It was my Yiayia who first exposed me to CNN. She was a big *Larry King Live* fan and personified appointment television viewing long before I understood the concept. When Larry's theme song began at 9 P.M., it sparked a level of excitement in my grandmother that could be rivaled only by a new bottle of Pinot Grigio. And if Larry's guest happened to be Suzanne Somers, well, holy shit, get out your party pants. While other kids my age were busy developing social skills, I sat wrapped in Yiayia's quilt watching Larry King interview Elizabeth Taylor and her jewelry. I started telling my Yiayia that I wanted to be like Larry when I grew up.

She told me to be patient, a virtue she one day explained to me in the car as she cut off a fire engine.

I figured that if I couldn't have Larry's job, maybe someday I'd at least be important enough to be a guest on his show. Afterward, I'd go upstairs to rehearse what I'd say to him during my first major prime-time interview:

LARRY: It's a pleasure to welcome to *Larry King Live* Jack Gray, the Academy Award–winning director of such films as *Herbie Goes Bananas and Kills His Family* and *The Sound of Music 2: Fraulein Maria Commits Adultery*.

ME: Hi, Larry, it's so good to be here. I love your eyeglass frames. Lou Dobbs was right. They are giving me an erection.

LARRY: Jack, I want to get to your illustrious movie career in a moment, but first I have to ask you about the story that has everyone buzzing: are you really having an affair with Jennie Garth?

ME: Now, Larry, you know better than to ask about my love life. How about we just take some calls? There must be someone on the line. Chattanooga, are you there?

LARRY: We'll get to calls in a minute, but I also need to ask you about that picture of you and Betty White in *People* magazine. That was quite unusual.

ME: What can I say, Larry? Underwear is overrated. But enough about me. Let's talk about you and Frank Sinatra. Did he tell you where Jimmy Hoffa is buried? He's in the trunk of your car, isn't he, Larry?

LARRY: We've got to take a break, but there's more to come
         with Jack Gray. Tomorrow night, President Clinton
         will be here. And on Thursday night, Mrs. Garrett
         from *The Facts of Life*. Don't go away.

There was never a question in my mind that I would grant
my first interview to Larry. Sure, the other TV giants would be
interested as well. But I knew if I went with Barbara Walters, I
would just end up in tears after she yelled at me for not knowing, if I were a tree, what tree I would be. Diane Sawyer might
not have made me cry, but I would have been too distracted by
her pouty lips and smooth legs. Same with Morley Safer.

During the commercials Larry and I would relax because, of
course, we would be buddies off-camera. We'd smoke cigarettes
and talk about our mutual friends like Jon Bon Jovi and Flor-
ence Henderson. Larry would regale me with stories about the
good old days—stories that all ended up with him sleeping with
Angie Dickinson.

If you read Larry's memoir, *My Remarkable Journey,* you'll see
that at least 75 percent of the anecdotes end with him and Ms.
Dickinson in a hotel room playing hide the kosher pickle. That's
before you get to the part where Larry recounts trying to get into
Katie Couric's pants. And the time Jessica Hahn—at the height
of the Jim and Tammy Faye Bakker scandal—played footsy with
Larry's crotch in the backseat of a limo. Not to mention the pas-
sage covering how, during the O. J. Simpson trial, Larry was
dating members of the defense AND the prosecution. It's a terrific read, even though it omits the time I saved his life during a
makeup room melee with Dr. Phil.

After the show Larry would invite me to dinner at the Palm.

"My treat," he'd say, a generous offer, to be sure, but one I would accept cautiously in light of my recent credit card dispute with Pat Sajak. We would have a corner booth, a power table befitting our clout and cufflinks. Larry would hold court as various celebrities came over to say hello. I'd invite Kelsey Grammer to join us for caviar as Larry urged Loni Anderson to remove her blouse.

It would be, I knew in my heart, a friendship that would endure. Vacations in Gstaad, afternoons of leisure in Beverly Hills, drinking lobster smoothies with Judge Judy. But it would be more than that. Larry would be my mentor. He would take me aside and explain the secret to his success. "Hard work is the key," he'd say. "That, and vibrating beds."

Fast forward to 2007. I was a new hire at CNN and still in awe of Larry King. I played it cool whenever I saw him in the hallway. And by "played it cool" I mean shrieked like a girl and peppered him with questions about Suzanne Somers. And no, I never broke into his studio late at night and sobbed at his desk. I don't know anything about that.

It's cliché to say Larry is an icon, but he is. The memorable moments are countless. Interviews with the biggest celebrities, debates among the most important politicians. And, of course, that time he made out with Marlon Brando. Beyond being an icon, though, Larry is a genuinely nice guy. Warm, with a terrific sense of humor, he is unpretentious for a man so rich he has a private army of monkey butlers. I got more comfortable seeing him around the building—I'd remain calm and say hello, and he'd say hello back. Not because he remembered who I was— I'm sure he didn't—more likely because he saw me eyeing his wallet.

Once, I wrote a blog post about him, just a tongue-in-cheek tribute. Someone printed it out and showed it to him just before he taped an interview about his book with Anderson. I heard them talking about it before the taping began; Larry was saying that he enjoyed the blog. When the taping was done, he asked Anderson to summon me down to the studio so he could meet me. I was beyond nervous. I'd said hello to him in the hallway before but this was a big deal. I was getting an audience with the King. Anderson introduced us and Larry said how much he liked the blog piece and asked me what other writing I had done and whether I ever considered writing professionally. I assumed he was high, but I was flattered nonetheless. He signed my copy of his book, "For Jack: A true talent. Good luck, Larry King." I don't know about talent—maybe he just autographed all of his books that way. Nevertheless, it's a prized possession of mine, resting in a spot of honor on my bookshelf.

One night in the fall of 2010, I managed to finagle an invitation to a party at Larry's house in Beverly Hills in celebration of a new book written by his senior executive producer, Wendy Walker. I had no business being there, but my friend Jason, a producer at *Larry King Live,* added my name to the guest list when no one was paying attention. Walking up to the house— let's be honest, it's a mansion—was surreal. I kept waiting for someone to turn me away but, amazingly, they let me in.

There I was in Larry King's foyer, which was the size of every house and apartment I'd ever lived in. There was a mix of CNN folks, friends of Larry, and some of his most frequent guests like Kathy Griffin, Bill Maher, and, yes, Suzanne Somers. I don't know how I resisted begging for an autographed ThighMaster.

As I wasn't driving, I loitered around the wine. If I was

going to pass out drunk anywhere on that trip to California, it was damn sure going to be Larry King's foyer. I'm hardly a wine connoisseur—I learned the hard way not to pair Chardonnay with Froot Loops—but even I noticed that the wine was being served in plastic cups instead of wineglasses. Given that this was a swanky Beverly Hills affair, I knew something was amiss. It turns out there was a miscommunication with the caterer, who hadn't showed up, and that left Larry and his wife, Shawn, scrambling to gather food and drinks for what must have been at least sixty people. Guests were rushing out to the store to buy wine and platters of meat. It was kind of refreshing to know that even in the heart of Beverly Hills, the parties weren't much different than the ones my family had growing up. Except no one was saying, "Go get the smelling salts and wake up your uncle."

The best part was when Larry and Shawn climbed halfway up the sweeping staircase to address the assembled guests. They each made heartfelt remarks about Wendy and her book, and then apologized for the lack of food. I was hoping for the green light to start rummaging through the kitchen cabinets, but no such permission was granted. That was OK. Larry and Shawn were so entertaining, I think everyone forgot about dinner. Looking up at the two of them on those grand stairs, I half-expected them to break out into song, like the Von Trapp children when their father sent them upstairs to bed in *The Sound of Music*.

Unfortunately, life was not all Rodgers and Hammerstein lyrics that year. Media critics were harping on the tired meme that CNN was in dire need of new direction. And while that was no doubt partially true, I found the repeated use of Larry King as Exhibit A to be a bit excessive. Yes, Larry's ratings were down, but the whole story line just felt harsh and excessive. It crystal-lized the cruel television reality that when you're hot you're hot, and when you're not, well, it never ends well.

Not that I'm one to talk about television loyalty. After all, how many TV shows had I written off as being past their prime? *Gossip Girl,* I'm looking in your direction. *Saturday Night Live,* I've been unfaithful. It's hypocritical for me to criticize anyone who turned against Larry. They viewed him as a brand, as an entity. But even if he was a lion in winter, I thought the group-think-media-echo-chamber-everyone-with-a-blog-has-to-shit-on-him bandwagon was tacky. The man was a cable television pioneer. His body of work as a long-format television host re-mains unrivaled. He deserved better.

The man who succeeded Larry, Piers Morgan, is an energetic interviewer, full of new style and what I believe is a phony En-glish accent. It's not his fault that the Larry King era had to come to an end. It's just that Larry King—the glasses, the suspenders, the occasionally jarring hair dye—connects me to my past. Not just to the hopes and dreams I once had of a career in television, but to the hours I spent watching his show with my grandpar-ents. Like Larry, they are not getting any younger.

It's sad to think about.

But Larry had a good run and now has an online show.

And my grandparents—they'll be fine. I gave them a Larry King coffee mug that I stole from the set.

TWITTER,
THY NAME IS WHALE PENIS

It was around the time that I explained why I was going to Los Angeles in October 2009—"Soleil Moon Frye invited me to a Twitter conference at the Kodak Theatre"—that my friends started to wonder what my life had become. It was as if I had never before flown cross-country to discuss social media with an eighties TV icon at a Hollywood landmark. They had forgotten about that night outside Whisky A Go Go and the woman I thought was Alan Alda.

Nevertheless, I was thrilled to go to L.A., a city I visit far too seldom. It wasn't until I arrived that I realized how much I'd missed its palm trees and poor air quality. The reason I don't go to Los Angeles more often is that I have a slight-to-moderate fear of flying. Luckily, I was distracted on the flight by the gentleman next to me, a man who—for reasons known only to his grocer and/or therapist—kept fiddling with a selection of deli meats.

Transcontinental salami aside, it was a terrific few days. I joined Ms. Moon Frye (call her Punky Brewster and she'll cut you) for a panel discussion of Twitter. I know, I know—people paying to go to a conference about Twitter? I didn't quite get it, either. But far be it from me to screw myself out of a free cross-country trip to In-N-Out Burger.

I wasn't always pro-Twitter. When I first heard about it, I was skeptical. I thought that it'd be fascinating for a week and then peak with an item on *Access Hollywood* that began with, "Lindsay Lohan announced on her Twitter page today that she failed her drug test." And, granted, that more or less actually happened. But on a broader level, I was wrong: Twitter is fun. At least it was at first. It seemed organic and enjoyable. When it became more widely publicized, it turned less fun.

At its worst moments Twitter felt like a forum filled with lunatics and trolls hiding behind anonymous screen names writing hateful, awful comments. Other times it seemed like a place populated only by people who spent their time begging celebrities for real-time acknowledgment. Then there were the celebrities and wannabe celebrities blathering on and on about nothing and addictively retweeting compliments about themselves. There is a reason why movie stars have publicists. They should not be allowed to have direct communication with the public. Scrolling through my Twitter feed devolved into the kind of thing that was only worth my time if I was on the toilet. Even then I had better things to do.

In the early days, though, it was much better. Twitter seemed perfect for people, like me, who were increasingly of the opinion that traditional forms of communication like phone calls and e-mails were taking up valuable time that could otherwise be spent watching *Oprah*. Twitter forces you to cram your thoughts into a maximum of 140 characters, 120 characters more interesting than my life actually is.

My Twitter username was @JackGrayCNN, which, in retrospect, was rather uninspired. I regret not going with my gut and choosing @OliveGardenBreadsticksGetMeHard or @MyFootIsAsleep. I figured my username represented the mix of personal and professional musings that I'd be sharing. That was if there was an interest. There were much bigger names at CNN already on Twitter. Anderson Cooper. Larry King. And I was no Larry King. Sure, I put on suspenders and shouted, "Wichita, you're on with Priscilla Presley," but that was between me and the other shoppers at Best Buy. And, despite the name I used to open credit card accounts, I'm no Anderson Cooper.

Twitter isn't for everyone. Many of my friends still don't understand the technology. That's fine. They never understood me anyway. Go ahead—build your careers, raise your families, donate your time to charitable causes. It's not my fault you think only of yourselves. I'm focused on the important things in life like tweeting when I sneeze and chronicling my war against Crocs.

There are the traditionalists for whom handwritten letters are still the preferred method of correspondence. For me, though, calligraphy on expensive stationery lacks the thoughtfulness and heartfelt sentiment of: "OMG thx for the $$

grandma. U r gr8. Can't w8 2 c u soon. Luv, Jack." At one point I considered cutting off all forms of communication except for Twitter. I mean, I have a phone, but all I get are calls from bill collectors and jilted lovers. (Ironically, not because I'm late on payments, but because I only date bill collectors.)

I signed up for a Twitter account in February of 2009, just a couple of months before Ashton Kutcher challenged CNN to a race to a million followers; a contest that, after much publicity, culminated with a middle-of-the-night sprint-to-the-finish and live Web cast. Sitting at home on my couch, I announced to my dog—who yawned and licked herself—that I was too good to pay any attention to such a publicity stunt. And then, of course, I sat in front of my computer for three hours.

As the moment arrived when Mr. Kutcher won, I became transfixed by my screen. He and his then wife, Demi Moore, were hosting some sort of victory party. There was laughter, there was shouting, there was . . . *holy shit is that Soleil Moon Frye?! What the hell is going on out there?!*

Besides rivaling Boutros Boutros-Ghali for the world's coolest name, Soleil Moon Frye—for those of you pretending to not know who she is—is the actress who rose to stardom playing lovable orphan Punky Brewster on the popular 1980s NBC sitcom of the same name. If you really don't know whom I'm talking about, well, I'm sorry you hate America.

Long before stars like the Olsen twins and Miley Cyrus came on the scene, there was Ms. Moon Frye. As a child, she was a staple of my weekday television viewing. Each afternoon I would put on my jean jacket, tie a brightly colored bandana around my head, and watch Punky get into new mischief.

During the commercials I would daydream about golden retrievers and elderly foster parents. After the show I would sit in my room, silently resenting Punky's best friend, Cherie (pronounced Cherry) Johnson, for living my dream: being named after produce. I've since shared my thoughts with Soleil about the episode during which Cherie gets stuck in a refrigerator. I'm not saying I wanted her to die. I'm just saying they could have left her in there a little longer.

It turns out, Ashton Kutcher runs a production company with Soleil Moon Frye's husband, Jason Goldberg. At the time, both couples were the best of friends—the Ricardos and the Mertzes of the Hollywood tech set—and hung out all the time and had dinners and watched *Dude, Where's My Car?* At least that's the way I pictured it when I was sitting at home, alone in the dark with the voices in my head. As if not being part of that clique wasn't bad enough, it turns out that Ashton is godfather to Soleil and Jason's children. Which raises the question: why is Soleil Moon Frye not *my* godmother? All it would take is one phone call: "Hi, Aunt Sue, sorry, but you're out and Punky Brewster is in. Don't ever call me again."

Amid all the buzz about Ashton's massive following, I realized that Punky, er—Soleil—was a Twitter powerhouse in her own right with, at the time, hundreds of thousands of followers, eventually more than a million. So, I wrote a few blog posts about her on the *Anderson Cooper 360°* Web site, and she saw them and got in touch with me. The rest is Twitter history. We're now best friends. BEST. FRIENDS. Deal with it, Demi Moore. (Years later I would meet Demi Moore a few times through Soleil. Once I ended up in a New York club, on top of a banquette, dancing to Rihanna's "S&M" and trying not to jostle Demi with my rhythmically challenged elbows.)

When you're best friends with Soleil Moon Frye, you get to have dinner with her and her posse in Hollywood. And when you're out to dinner with Soleil Moon Frye and her posse in Hollywood, you get to hear anecdotes like, "No, MC Hammer can't make it."

Not every celebrity on Twitter is as delightful as Ms. Moon Frye. *Cough* Star Jones. Ms. Jones, former cohost of *The View*, took umbrage with—and by that I mean went bananas—a few tweets I wrote about her. I was surfing around on Twitter one morning and noticed Ms. Jones had, say, 9,000 followers and I had, say, 6,000 followers. For some reason it struck me as funny that we were only a few thousand apart because, you know, she used to be on a huge television show. I tweeted: "I can't get over that Star Jones has more followers than me." And all the responses I got from people were along the lines of, "Haha, you can overtake her." Amused by the feedback and because I'm socially awkward and had nothing better to do, I tweeted, "I'm enlisting Anderson to help me close the gap with Star Jones. It's bad enough I didn't get that job cohosting *The View*." Obviously a joke, right? Certainly not something anyone would take seriously. Certainly not Star Jones who, one would assume, has better things to do. Well, one would assume wrong. My tweets, followed by a tweet from Anderson—"please follow @JackGrayCNN so he stops complaining that Star Jones has more followers than he does"—provoked Star into a bit of a Twitter rage.

Her first response, "Now that's just tacky . . . and you know

it. LOL," didn't make me too nervous. She didn't seem to love what I wrote, but I figured she was just mildly annoyed and would let it go. But just to be safe, I tweeted out: "For the record, I have nothing against Star Jones. She is lovely, talented & smart. Just a random celebrity I picked to try to catch up to." Lovely. Talented. And. Smart. End of story, as far as I was concerned. Oh no, Star Jones was just getting warmed up. She maintained a steady stream of tweets over the next few hours, "what's up with people comparing their number of followers to mine? ya'll give me far tooooo much energy. I'm not even on TV everyday." (I resisted the urge to reply, "and thank God for that.") She continued, "I'm on [sic] chillin in my own life talking on twitter like everyone else. Don't make me use these 'Haters' as 'Motivators' and step it up! LOL." So, apparently, I was now a "hater," though I found that characterization less irksome than her continued use of "LOL." Don't even get me started on people who use "LOL." Just promise that if I ever use it, you'll kill me.

Star's inability-to-take-a-joke tweets continued. My favorite line from her was: "Made it safe and sound. Unloading the car now. We'll be thinking of Anderson, his producer and the rest while grilling fish this evening." Grilling fish? I was lost. Was that supposed to be an insult? Because all it did was motivate me to go to Whole Foods and buy some salmon. But, at least, I thought, my ill-conceived born-out-of-what-I-thought-was-obviously-good-natured-humor Twitter War was over. I pictured Star out in the Hamptons, forgetting about Twitter and doing whatever else it is that she does. Probably going to the grocery store and scolding people who don't recognize her.

Anyway, that was Friday. On Monday—three days since my last tweet about Star, three days since I considered the whole stupid thing to be over, three days since I'd even thought about her—the episode resurfaced. My grace period to send her a bouquet of Payless shoes having apparently expired, Star complained about me to a producer at CNN who, in turn, contacted my boss. Sweet. Mother. Of. God. Somebody. Shoot. Me. Please. Twenty-eight years old, barely able to make the rent for my miniscule studio apartment, and Star Jones, lounging out in the Hamptons with her grilled fish, was now messing with my job. All because of a few silly, mindless tweets. Fortunately, my boss, who realized it was much ado about nothing, had my back and told me not to worry about it.

My only real regret from the whole thing is not warning others to beware of the Wrath of Jones. About six months after her little dustup, I noticed a tweet from Bravo star Andy Cohen mentioning how he was having lunch at New York's chic Monkey Bar and saw "Star Jones and her weave." Now, anyone who knows Andy Cohen would know he was joking. For fuck's sake, the man produces the *Real Housewives* franchise, he hosts the Housewives reunion shows on Bravo—his business is based on weaves. His tweet wasn't a shot at Star, it was just an opportunity to mention a weave. But Star, the Mayor of Crazytown, fired back. I had to look away. If you're ever tempted to make a Twitter joke about Star Jones, I'd suggest you reconsider and find a more relaxed subject, like the Taliban.

My other celebrity encounters on Twitter were more pleasant. Star Jones was the complete opposite of, say, Mariel Hemingway, the actress and granddaughter of Ernest Hemingway.

Besides being gorgeous—and not losing her temper when I call in the middle of the night quoting *For Whom the Bell Tolls*—Mariel is relaxed and affable. We made plans to get together while I was in Los Angeles, as she was also speaking at the Twitter conference. So, the day arrives and we meet up and it's all Hollywood kisses-on-the-cheek and smiles, and I'm just soaking it all in and then—insert sound of a record player screeching to a halt—she introduces me to Bob. Bob her boyfriend. I don't know how to describe Bob except for maybe that you'd take that guy who hosts *Survivor,* add in Dr. Phil, merge them into one person, and give that person an assload of caffeine.

Now, to be fair, Bob probably hadn't had any caffeine. He was, and is, the picture of heath—another of his faults. Nevertheless, Bob was enthusiastic. I think the conversation went something like, "Hi, Bob, I'm Jack. Nice to meet you." Bob replied, "Hey-so-I've-got-these-two-reality-show-deals-in-development-one-is-with-Fox-and-the-other-we're-still-shopping-around-but-Adrien-Brody-is-attached-to-executive-produce-and-it's-going-to-be-me-taking-five-guys-out-into-the-desert-and-I'm-really-going-to-work-the-shit-out-of-them-because-like-this-is-what-people-want-and-it-isn't-just-about-fitness-it's-about-life-you-know-what-I'm-talking-about-this-isn't-just-about-being-in-shape-it's-being-who-you-are-and-finding-yourself-and-then-we're-going-to-a-sweat-lodge-and-then-I'm-going-to-take-you-rafting-in-Africa-and-then-I'm-going-to-design-a-vitamin-plan-just-for-you-and-there-will-be-a-winner-but-everyone-is-really-a-winner-and-you-know-look-at-me-I'm-in-great-shape-I'm-the-real-deal-no-one-has-ever-done-this-before-the-network-is-superexcited-and-this-is-going-to-be-huge."

Oh, Bob, the only thing that's going to be huge is the dose of Valium I'm taking when I get back to my hotel.

But you can't say Bob doesn't care. He asked about my health just twenty minutes after meeting me. I must not have been doing a good job of masking my glow of red wine and Hostess apple pies.

"Have you had your minerals yet today?"

"Excuse me?" I asked.

"Your minerals," he repeated.

"Um, well, I took a multivitamin this morning," I lied.

He shook his head in disapproval and produced a small plastic tube of what appeared to be water.

"Here, take this," he said.

"What is it?" I asked, looking to Mariel for reassurance.

"It's fresh from the ocean, loaded with minerals," Bob explained.

"OK, well, sure," I said as he handed me the tube. As I drank the liquid—and dribbled some down my shirt—Bob said those magic words: "It's good for you . . . it's from whale penis." The words reverberated inside my head in slow motion: WHAAAALLE. PEEEEENIS. Unfuckingbelieveable, Bob. I might as well have blown Moby-Dick himself.

Whale penis notwithstanding, my foray into the Twitterverse—and, yes, that's a word because Ashton Kutcher said so—continued and led to discussions with friends and family. There was the obvious question, "What *is* Twitter?"—always said in a tone of voice that made clear whoever was asking had decided he or she didn't like it. Then there was, "Do I really *need* Twitter?" Of course you don't *need* Twitter. Just like you don't need Facebook. (I don't use Facebook. No one wants to look at pictures of your wedding. No one even wants to go to your wedding.) Then there were those who would outright mock it, "Oh are you going to put this on *Twitter*? Don't *tweet* about me. Are you tweeting *right now*? Everyone look at Jack, he's *tweeting*!" No, sorry, I'm actually not tweeting right now. I'm texting a stranger I met online.

What bothers me is how news organizations pander to people using social media. It's one thing to say, "Hey, here's our Twitter address, follow us for breaking news alerts." It's quite another to solicit tweets and Facebook comments from random people and then read them on-air as if they're crucial. You might as well just say, "Our show sucks but stay tuned because we might say your name on TV." Organic, authentic Twitter interaction between anchors and viewers can't hurt and is worth trying, but overly strategized network initiatives give me a headache. Social this, social that. Please. I'm in the most coveted demographic for television advertisers, and the day I meet a contemporary who references a viewer tweet as a pivotal moment in his or her television viewing experience is the day I let Piers Morgan pierce my nipples with a rusty paperclip. I mean, really, who tweets a TV network? OK, fine, I've tweeted to the Lifetime network before. It was when Roseanne Barr had a reality show set on a macadamia-nut farm. In case you missed it, Lifetime had to pixilate her vagina during the *first episode*. The first fucking episode. That's how rich Roseanne is. She just doesn't give a shit about putting on underwear. Roseanne is also one of the craziest and most frequent celebrity Twitter users out there. Rampage after rampage. I followed her for a long time before I got tired of her clogging up my screen. She's a comedic genius, but that doesn't translate on Twitter. Occasionally she made sense, but often her rants were so insane that it was as if someone had pixilated her brain.

Yet, as much as Twitter is a side dish to the entrée of actual television programming, I acknowledge that it's been a significant factor in my career. For reasons unknown to me, I was placed on Twitter's mysterious-but-coveted Suggested User List, which drove hundreds of thousands of followers, most of whom were spammers, to my account. Suddenly I was *somebody* at CNN. People knew my name and wanted to talk to me. It was all rather delightful until I realized many of them just wanted me to tweet about them and plug their latest project. And the moniker of The Twitter Guy grew tired. Not that I didn't milk my newfound "clout," making some new and quite wonderful friends. I even parlayed some on-camera gigs. That part of it was exciting, but I realized that Twitter followers didn't necessarily equal influence. That I have a big platform underscores how Twitter has given us a skewed sense of who—and what—is important. Who the hell am I and why should anyone care about what I tweet? And the same goes for 99.9% of Twitter users, including many of the legitimately famous ones. So much of it is just noise. People used to talk just to hear themselves talk. Now they tweet just to see themselves tweet. Sometimes, myself included.

That said, Twitter has done some genuine good in the world—there's no arguing that—including the Ashton Kutcher–CNN contest, which raised awareness and money for an admirable charity, Malaria No More. And social media has been an important tool for prodemocracy movements. That's reason enough for Twitter to keep going, to say nothing of its ability to bring attention to important stories and causes, and to connect people around the world.

But, relax, I'm not saying you have to start tweeting or hanging out with Soleil Moon Frye or feuding with Star Jones or drinking whale semen with Mariel Hemingway.

I'm just saying that if you're against Twitter, you support the spread of malaria.

TALES FROM THE GREEN ROOM

I didn't mean to almost pee on Maria Shriver. It wasn't really my fault, for two reasons. First, my desk at CNN is far away from the bathroom in the massive Time Warner Center, nearly the distance of an entire city block. Second, the medical community says that I'm supposed to drink three liters of water a day, which I try to do. A quasi-hypochondriac, I am convinced that I'm going to drop dead any moment. The least I can do is stay hydrated.

So there I was one night, around eight-thirty or so, when I hit the limit at my desk. I couldn't hold it any longer. I had to get to the bathroom and I had to get there fast. Rushing past my colleagues, I did that awkward walk-run combo that people do when they have to use the restroom urgently. Trying to act casual only makes the situation more obvious. No one limps briskly to pick up delivery food.

As I turned the corner from the newsroom into the long hallway that leads to the staff bathroom, I knew I wasn't going to make it. I had to go to Plan B, the green room. Everyone from President Clinton to Queen Latifah—though, unfortunately, never at the same time—has passed through the CNN green room. Staffers—especially low-level staffers like me—aren't supposed to use those bathrooms. But that's a rule that's neither especially followed nor enforced, which is great for us but not so great for whatever Real Housewife is sitting on the sofa when you emerge from the bathroom after taking a dump. Not that that's ever happened to me. Most of the staffers who use the green room lavatories do so only during off-hours late at night. I do have one friend who, after a bowel emergency of unusual magnitude, reported back that he had made it into the green room bathroom just in time to do a "Jackson Pollock" all over the toilet.

Fortunately, I only had to pee. All was quiet on the seventh floor. This was back in the day when *Larry King Live* was still on the air, which was mainly broadcast from Los Angeles. We always knew when Larry was in New York—during the U.N. General Assembly he would round up many of the world's dictators for a kind of Despot Old Home Week—but I knew that night he was in L.A. There was no reason to think he had any guests hanging around on the seventh floor. If anything, he might have a guest booked in a smaller "flash-cam" studio—a tiny room with just a robotically controlled camera and a piece of the famous *Larry King Live* backdrop—but those are all down on the fifth floor. So, as I rounded the corner and into the green room, unbuttoning my fly and preparing to whip out my penis, I didn't expect to see Maria Shriver, then the First Lady of

California. But there she was—no aides, no entourage, no one—standing in the green room, talking on her cellphone. We stared at each other for a second. "Oh my God, I'm so sorry," I said. Normally I don't gush, but for some reason—maybe it was my undone fly—I just started blabbering. "It's-so-nice-to-see-you-I'm-such-a-big-admirer-if-you're-talking-to-Arnold-please-tell-him-I-said-hi." I'm surprised she didn't hit some sort of panic button. Instead, she told the person on the phone to hold on, extended her hand, said how nice it was to meet me, and asked me my name. Whether that was to be polite or to pass along to her security detail, I don't know.

Politicians and their spouses are green room regulars. The late Elizabeth Edwards, whom I met at my old station in Boston—which didn't so much have a green room as a staff conference room with a broken TV—was charming. Her former husband is another story. America might forgive a politician who cheats on his wife, but not one who cheats on his cancer-stricken wife. Rod Blagojevich made me sad, too, though for different reasons. I saw the disgraced Illinois governor in the hallway outside the green room after he'd appeared with Larry. Blagojevich's lips said "I'm innocent," but his man-bangs said "not so fast." Barney Frank holds the distinction as the only member of Congress to bring me to the verge of tears. I had seated him in our makeshift Boston green room and informed him that he would be going on set in about ten minutes. He started to berate me for daring to make him wait and then went off about how he wouldn't be doing local TV if he hadn't known my anchorman for a long time. At that point I didn't know that the congressman had a reputation for being self-important and difficult. I pleaded with him to stay. If he left—as he was threatening to do—I'd be stuck with a ten-minute hole on live television. Fortunately, he did the show but, to this day, whenever I hear a producer book Barney Frank, I tell him or her to not be surprised if he throws a tantrum.

But for every nightmare encounter with an ornery congressman is a chance meeting with a courteous movie star. I was walking past the green room one day at CNN when out came none other than Robert Redford. I was so excited I damn near started to hump his leg. At least I didn't undo my fly, though as I introduced myself to him, I gave him one of those handshakes that went on just a bit too long. You know the kind, where the person looks down at his hand, as if to say, "You can fucking let go now." I'm just glad I didn't start singing "The Way We Were," though I may have snuck in one of those little nose salutes from *The Sting*.

Then there was the time Angelina Jolie swooped in to do an interview with Larry. And "swoop" is the only word to describe the fanfare with which she entered. I should point out heads of state and other dignitaries are frequently on the seventh floor. Never in my memory has the hallway been blocked off. The only time I've seen it happen was with Angelina Jolie. It wasn't her decision. In-house security wanted to keep everyone away from the area she'd be walking through. I'd be damned if that was going to stop me. A few of us leaned around a corner to catch a glimpse. I was the only one shameless enough to shout out "Hello, Angelina!" when she arrived. She waved back and said hello, smiling. She did not, however, adopt me.

The only person—besides Betty White—whom I ever sought out for a photograph at CNN was Liza Minnelli. Liza with a Z was not getting out of the building without meeting Jack with a J. Ms. Minnelli was in the green room having her makeup done for *The Joy Behar Show*. I barged in—I mean, knocked politely. I announced that I was a friend of Kathy Griffin, whom Liza knows, and she broke into a wide smile and said, in that classic Liza voice, "Aww, really? That's swell, come on over here," like she was talking to the ghost of Sammy Davis, Jr. I was in gay heaven and, as such, took on Liza's mannerisms. All of a sudden, I was in a slinky *Cabaret* pose, which works for Liza, but not so much for a pear-shaped male.

I also dropped Kathy's name to meet Olympic skater Johnny Weir. He was in the building to appear on *Larry King Live*. I'd rooted for him in the Vancouver games; I thought it was lame how the skating world seemed to shun him for his flamboyance. Kathy texted Johnny to tell him I would be coming downstairs to meet him. He was polite, but it was one of those let-down moments, when you're excited to meet someone and they don't meet the threshold of feigning interest. Some celebrities meet people and make them feel like they're the only person in the room. Jimmy Fallon has that ability. I introduced him to my sister, and he couldn't have been greater, even when my sister nervously responded to his "nice to meet you" with "you're welcome." But Johnny Weir didn't quite have that. He was nice, but, as so often happens, I only got as far as "Hi, my name is Jack, I work upstairs for Anderson Coop—" before he cut me off and said, "Oh my God, I'm such a huge fan, can you go tell him I want to meet him?" Now I root for Russia.

On the other end of the spectrum, while sitting in a CNN makeup chair, actor John Leguizamo could not have been more eager to talk to me, especially about the link between baldness remedies and erectile dysfunction—a topic that incidentally, I had not brought up.

The "actor" Fabio didn't even make it to the green room in Boston. The ladies in the building swarmed him in the lobby, where he picked them up, one by one, in his arms and posed for photographs. And if you're wondering what kind of show I was producing where I was booking people like Fabio, so am I.

I was giddy to meet Nora Ephron. I didn't think my crush on her could be any stronger until she sent my anchorman in Boston a handwritten thank-you note. I'm sure I stole it and stuffed it into my boxer shorts.

My grandparents equipped me with a Greek phrase to greet Arianna Huffington with when she arrived in Boston for an interview. Relying on them was a risk, since by that time their Greek was rather rusty. They often confused "Hello" with "Get over here, you chubby rascal."

I've never met Diane Keaton, one of my favorite actresses. Her green room door was closed when she was at CNN, so I couldn't weasel my way in there with a fake excuse. If I had, I don't know what I would have said. I probably just would have curtsied and asked her to marry me.

The best might have been Jerry Seinfeld. He is arguably my favorite New Yorker of all time. I worship him like the comedy god he is. Seinfeld was for me what *I Love Lucy* was for my mother. I'd seen him around the city before and I'd seen him do stand-up, but when I heard he was in the building to appear on *Larry King Live,* I knew I had to get a meet-and-greet. I poked my head into his green room door during the show. I saw a guy I knew I recognized, though I couldn't think of his name. Like the jackass I am, I said, "Hey, you're the guy from that movie, the documentary about that comedian." It was George Shapiro, Seinfeld's legendary manager, who looked at me like I was an idiot. "You mean the documentary *Comedian* about Jerry Seinfeld?" Yeah, that's the one. It shows how nice Team Seinfeld is that I still got my meet-and-greet. And it shows how nice I am that I didn't pee on anyone.

THIS DOESN'T CHANGE ANYTHING

I don't know why the sailor didn't use the bathroom before we left South Beach. Maybe he did. Maybe he'd "broken the seal" and already had to go again. What I do know is that ten minutes into the drive back to Fort Lauderdale he was urinating into a beer bottle, which he then tossed out the window. It was 4 A.M. and we were in a minivan that was moving much too fast. There were five of us: four members of the United States Navy, whom I had known for four hours, and me. They were in town for Fleet Week. I was in town for vacation. My friend Mark wasn't sched-uled to join me until the following day, so I was alone when I met the sailors at a downtown Lauderdale bar. Beers were con-sumed. Adventures were hatched. They wanted to see Miami. Let's go, I said. The problem was that it was a Tuesday and nightlife wasn't exactly booming. We ended up at News Cafe, the twenty-four-hour restaurant Gianni Versace had visited just before he was murdered, a macabre piece of fashion trivia that had no resonance with my new friends. As if running off with a bunch of drunken sailors on a Tuesday wasn't pointless enough, they were straight.

Back safely, amazingly, in Fort Lauderdale, the sailors dropped me off at the condo where I was staying. I watched the sun rise over a Navy ship anchored off the beach and went to sleep. When Mark arrived the next day, he grinned with pride as I recounted my unusual night. Mark and I had grown up together. We had worked in a video store/tanning parlor together. We had gotten drunk together. He's also much smarter than me, went to an excellent college, and built an impressive career for himself. And, of the two of us, he is the bigger partier, never letting anything come between him and a Coors Light. Jumping into a van with strangers I met at a bar was hardly my trademark. Mark knew I was more likely to be found at the beachfront Hooters, doing a crossword puzzle and eating my weight in curly fries.

At the time, Mark lived in New York and I in Boston. The distance had allowed me to take cover behind our infrequent visits. I had been plagued by depression off and on since college, but I hadn't told him. There's no need to tell him, I convinced myself. I'm on medication. He'll be worried. I'm not drunk enough. I had a thousand reasons. But the real reason, the only reason, was that I was embarrassed. I felt weak. I felt defective.

I can't drink as much as Mark, though I try my best to keep up. That's what I was doing in Lauderdale on the night I told him. Few emotional walls can withstand three bottles of cheap champagne. "I have something to tell you," I said.

"OK," he said.

"I hope you don't think of me differently."

"I won't. Just tell me."

"I'm depressed. Like, really depressed. Actual depression."

"Wow. Really?"

"Yes. I'm taking antidepressants. I've been on them since college."

He could have downplayed it. He could have changed the subject. He could have coddled me. Instead, Mark said exactly what I needed to hear, "What can I do to help?"

We talked for hours. We ordered more cheap champagne. We toasted our friendship.

The next day we went to a grocery store. We saw a gay couple in the parking lot, then another gay couple inside the store, and another gay couple as we got back into the car. "I didn't realize there were so many gay guys in Fort Lauderdale," he said. Not in a negative way. Just an observation. But still.

Gulp.

"Yeah, me neither," I said.

Maybe the next trip.

Three years would pass before I would tell Mark that I was gay. I told him the same night I told my mom and my sister. I had to tell them. I wanted to tell them. They were the people closest to me. I was twenty-eight and had wasted precious years. But I couldn't bring myself to call them on the phone. I was too scared. Scared they would react poorly. Scared I would not be able to speak the words.

Instead, I wrote them each an e-mail from my desk at CNN. Surely, I had other things to be doing at that moment. But it was as if I had gone into gay labor. I had been carrying this *thing* around inside me. I knew I was getting close. And then all of a sudden my gay water broke. I closed my eyes and clicked "send."

My mom called five minutes later. When I was little, I would put on a trench coat and eyeglasses with no lenses to try to get her attention while she cooked. If that didn't cause her to stop whatever she was doing and focus on me, I would leave and return draped in an afghan, wearing a flapper hat and carrying a wand made of tinfoil. My father once called me a mama's boy. He didn't mean it as a compliment, but he was right.

My sister beeped in while I was talking to my mom. Both were crying. Not, they were quick to say, because I was gay, but because I had felt unable to share that part of my life with them. Both offered unconditional support and said they'd love me until the end of time. I was relieved, even though they were quoting "Paradise by the Dashboard Light."

Mark texted me shortly after I hung up the phone. "Got your e-mail. Love you. Let's get dinner." I was nervous. Informing your straight best friend that you're gay is difficult enough by e-mail. But talking it over in person was not something I'd planned on doing in the short term. I thought maybe we'd get around to discussing it in six months or, perhaps, never. But two hours later Mark greeted me with a hug at Pete's Tavern on East 18th Street. And like that night in Fort Lauderdale, he said what I needed to hear: "This doesn't change anything."

And he was right.

Two days after I told her I was gay, I received a card in the mail from my mother.

I can only imagine how difficult this was for you and how much courage it took for you to finally, openly and honestly, tell me that you're gay. I want you to know that my only sadness is that you, for so long, had to keep from sharing this important piece of who you are simply because you thought I'd react in an unhappy, disappointed way. Nothing, my dear son, could be further from the truth. I love you even more, if that's at all possible.

There are three things I keep in the bottom drawer of my dresser: my passport, my birth certificate, and that card.

I hate surprises. And I don't much like houseguests. A combination of the two is something in which I have no interest. One would think my sister, Rose, who has known me her entire life, and my friend Liz, who knows me nearly as well, would realize that showing up at my one-bedroom apartment for an unannounced weekend visit would be a bad idea. Then again, perhaps I was naïve to think they were aware of how much I valued spending time undisturbed. Liz was the person who thought it would be a good idea—on a day I was home with the flu—to dispatch to my apartment something called a get-well chicken-gram. A get-well chicken-gram involves a stranger dressed in a head-to-toe chicken suit ringing the buzzer at your apartment, hollering "Delivery!" into the intercom, and scaring the shit out of you when you answer the door because you think the chicken is a spree killer.

Rose knows not to send me anything that involves someone clucking out a jingle in my hallway. Over the years, she had transformed from my childhood antagonist into a caring, thoughtful adult. If she has a fault, it's that she's too caring, too willing to give people the benefit of the doubt. And though she's appalled by my New York media industry cynicism, she's unfailingly supportive. Her support had reached such a level that she decided her visit to New York would include treating me to a proper gay night on the town. At least her well-intentioned, misinformed idea of one. "Let's go to that piano bar in your old neighborhood. And I want to go clubbing, too." I asked if she had me confused with someone else, someone who had even the slightest interest in doing anything besides watching *Frasier* reruns on the Hallmark Channel.

It wasn't just that Rose wanted to go out. She always wanted to go out when she was in New York. This was different. This wasn't her suggesting we go to a movie. It wasn't her asking me to get tickets to *Saturday Night Live*. It wasn't even really her wanting to go out to a bar. This was my sister trying to be a part of my life, trying to understand who I was and the world I lived in. I owed it to her—I owed it to myself—to let her in.

So we sang. We went to Marie's Crisis in the West Village and sang "Tomorrow" from *Annie* and "Do-Re-Mi" from *The Sound of Music,* just as we had done as kids. Then we went to a gay club called Splash and danced underneath a fog machine, which we had not done as kids. Rose said everyone was friendly, I said everyone was on crystal meth. She marveled at the strobe light, I checked my watch. When we returned to my apartment, Rose decided she'd overdone it on show tunes and tequila. I spent the rest of the night emptying vomit out of a fruit bowl. We had officially bonded.

My father knows I'm gay. I think. He's never asked and I've never told. He's a Republican—albeit a Massachusetts Republican—and gay issues are something we've never discussed. If he wonders why I've never brought a girlfriend to Christmas dinner, he keeps that to himself.

But he knows. He has to know. For a long time I wasn't sure. Our conversations revolved around a fixed set of topics—the price of gasoline, the weather, and the Red Sox—and never went deeper. It had taken the better part of a decade following my parents' divorce to salvage a stable relationship with my father, and I think both of us were content to keep things simple.

Years passed. Friends told me to tell him. My shrink told me to tell him. But it was a conversation I didn't want to have. It was a conversation I didn't need to have. I didn't have a boyfriend. I wasn't dating. I was gay but had no life to share. I told myself that if my dad ever asked me, I would answer honestly. But I hoped he wouldn't ask. Even though I didn't own a car, I much preferred discussing the price of gasoline.

Then late one night in June 2011 the New York legislature passed the legalization of same-sex marriage. We covered it extensively on CNN and I noted the news on my Twitter page. Fucking Twitter. The next morning I had an e-mail from my father.

I have read with interest your twitters about the historic vote in New York. Human rights issues are indeed important and gay rights are certainly one of them. Your employers over the years should be grateful for your humanity and empathy. You make your family proud! Love, Your Father

For a moment I wondered if his e-mail had been hacked. It was such an unexpected message, by far the most meaningful gesture he had ever made toward me. I wish I could say I did not squander the opportunity. I wish I couldn't say I wrote back only "good vote" and hoped that he wouldn't reply. But I did. And he didn't.

My dad knows that I'm gay. I think. And someday I will tell him.

Just not today.

THEY SAY THE NEON CARBS ARE BRIGHT ON BROADWAY

I've never won a Tony Award. Not for my one-man show, *Nice to Meet You, Now Please Get Out of My Bed;* not for my burlesque tribute to Angela Lansbury, *Murder, She Wrote . . . All Night Long.* Nothing.

I'm at a loss, frankly, as to why I've been passed over. It's not as if I'm a diva. I go out of my way to encourage audience participation. I don't care what the critics say, folks in the mezzanine love being showered with diet pills. The only reason I can think of for this theatrical injustice—aside from the unpleasantness with that jar of Nutella—is that the Broadway establishment didn't like my original number "Any Day You Don't Blow Your Shrink Is a Good Day."

OK, fine, that was all in my head—a wet dream set to the score of *Gypsy.* I've never been on Broadway or onstage, unless you count karaoke bars. And I really hope you don't because what Fleetwood Mac doesn't know won't hurt them. My friend Kathy Griffin had never been on Broadway, either, until March of 2011. She arrived in New York several days in advance of the opening of her brilliantly titled one-woman show, *Kathy Griffin Wants a Tony*, and, trust me, she wanted that Tony. I took a week off from work to make time for what I knew was going to be a once-in-a-lifetime experience. As we always did, Kathy and I met up in her hotel suite to chat into the wee hours while devouring a cookie cake. There's a place in New York called Insomnia Cookies, a late-night bakery that I'm pretty sure is just a bunch of NYU stoners sitting around a dorm room with a hot plate and a microwave. Whatever they're doing, we loved it. You call up and order a cookie cake at 1 A.M. and a half-hour later someone—the delivery people range from twenty-something hipsters to elderly drifters—shows up at your place with fourteen inches of warm delight.

I'd been backstage at Kathy's live shows around the country before—I may or may not have gotten my hands on Bette Midler's headdress at Caesars Palace—but backstage on Broadway was different. It was everything you'd imagine it to be, only much shittier. Backstage on Broadway is a dump. No wonder Bette and Cher and Céline play Vegas, with modern dressing rooms the size of upper-middle-class homes. Broadway theaters are old and smell and have wires and pipes sticking out all over the place.

Still, it was a hell of a treat to spend that eight-day run with Kathy hanging out at the Belasco Theatre on West 44th Street. The first night we arrived, friends and admirers of hers had sent flowers and edibles along with good-luck notes. My favorite was a life-size chocolate leg from someone named John. No one knew who John was, but that didn't stop me from eating it. I started with the toes, which was creepy on multiple levels. But, there was no way I was getting my mouth around that chocolate thigh. I was halfway through gnawing on the foot on the afternoon Rosie O'Donnell came backstage to say hi to Kathy. I had never met Rosie before. Since flattery works every time, she won me over with "Who's this cute guy?" My ego, however, was brought back to reality when Rosie announced that she'd recently lost some weight. It turned out she weighed less than I did.

After the show Rosie took us out for dinner to a place in Hell's Kitchen on the West Side of Manhattan. She had a posse that included her on-again-off-again girlfriend, who didn't say a word. She also brought actresses Chloë Sevigny and Natasha Lyonne, the latter of whom was said to be newly clean after a well-publicized struggle with drugs. Naturally, that caught my attention. I didn't need a junkie monopolizing the breadbasket. Been there, done that.

It was one of those dinners when I was thinking to myself, "What the hell am I doing here?" But I was grateful that Kathy wanted me around. I didn't know what to talk about with Chloë Sevigny. She's one of those celebrities whom I certainly had heard of, but I hadn't a clue as to what films or shows she'd been in. Kind of like Sienna Miller. I know she dated Jude Law and he cheated on her with his kids' nanny, or she cheated on him with the nanny, or she was the nanny, or something. But I don't know anything about her film career. And, no, Sienna Miller was not at dinner, I was just trying to make a point.

Later, after Googling Chloë Sevigny on my iPhone while I

was in the bathroom, I learned that she was on the HBO show *Big Love*. But since I was neither an expert on polygamy nor Bill Paxton, I turned my attention to Natasha Lyonne. Unfortunately, while I had no reason to doubt she was clean, I realized it was best I not bother her with conversation and let her focus on keeping her head out of her mashed potatoes.

Other dinners were also awkward. Rachael Ray came to the show one night and afterward took us out to a fancy restaurant in Tribeca. I knew that I shouldn't be there. First, I was in Tribeca. A good rule is that I'm not cool enough to be in any neighborhood where Robert De Niro owns a hotel. Second, nowhere on the menu did I see the words "basket of chicken tenders." I ordered what I thought would be my safest bet, some sort of beef dish with French fries. In the meantime the chef—as chefs do when I'm dining with celebrities but never, as it happens, when I'm dining with my grandparents at Applebee's—started sending out all kinds of complimentary appetizers that looked liked they had baked-in attitude problems. I declined Kathy's offer of duck con-whatever and stuck my hand into my man-purse for a fistful of cheddar Goldfish crackers.

The meals arrived, and my concerns were realized. I had envisioned a slab of medium-rare beef the size of a Honda Civic, but the restaurant had envisioned an overcooked morsel festooned—trust me, that is the only word to describe it—with garnishes I did not recognize and a sauce that could only be described as mucus. The French fries were not piled high and deep, or, as I prefer, in their own novelty souvenir bucket. There were precisely four French fries sticking out of—wait for it—a piece of bone marrow. Now, I don't know whose bone marrow it was or why there were French fries sticking out of it. I didn't even know that was an accepted culinary practice. Apparently there was some organ-donor fine print on the menu that I missed. Next time I hear people talking about a patient needing bone marrow, I'm giving them the address of that fucking restaurant. Rachael and Kathy fought over the check, Kathy ended up picking up the tab—which was like $800—for the meal. And her dish didn't even come with bone marrow.

We walked back to the Trump Soho hotel that night, trying to digest our expensive dinner and the reality that our voices would never sound as smoky as Rachael Ray's. Everything was fine until we got into the elevator. For some reason, even though I'd been in that elevator countless times, I got disoriented when it stopped to let people off on the way up to Kathy's floor. As the doors closed, I panicked in the way that someone who has had too much wine panics. Thinking we were missing our stop, I screamed and threw my hand out to try to stop the doors from closing. The good news is that I got my hand in there; the bad news is that the doors didn't open back up. They crushed my fingers, trapping them. The pain was excruciating. I yelped, "Yowser!"—a curiously benign and old-timey expression for a situation so painful and horrifying that everyone else in the elevator feared I had been maimed. It couldn't have lasted more than thirty seconds but felt, as those experiences tend to feel, like hours. Kathy just started shouting, "OhMyGodOhMyGod-OhMyGod," and kept hitting the "alarm" button that rings a bell and accomplishes nothing. I was less worried about broken bones than the elevator moving again and shearing my hand off. Donald Trump had done enough damage to the country. He wasn't getting my fingers.

The elevators did not resume motion. After considerable

effort and agony I pried my fingers out of the doors' vice grip. They looked chewed up and hurt to move, but didn't quite feel broken. As soon as we got to Kathy's room, I stuck my hand in a bucket of ice, where it stayed for the next two hours. After determining that I would not be forever prevented from carrying her purse, she began mocking me for saying "yowser" by dancing around, doing jazz hands, and singing "Hello My Ragtime Gal." Apparently, after I said "yowser," my mouth opened up into what she for weeks after would call my "silent cry," like I was moaning in pain but unable to make a sound. In retrospect, it was all rather pathetic and funny, though I now have about as much trust in elevator door sensors as I do in French fries served in bone marrow.

As much as those eight nights were heady times—what with the celebrity dinners and elevator mishaps—I needed to remind myself that it wasn't real life. At least not my real life. It was Kathy's life. It was important that my non-Broadway-headlining friends knew I wasn't abandoning them while she was in town, so I bought my pals Mark and Alyssa—newlyweds, the poor bastards—tickets to see the show for their wedding present. I took a photo of Mark and Kathy backstage. They posed like a prom picture, which was cute. Mark texted me after they left, "Thanks again. Please apologize to her for my erection." (He was joking, but believe me, she would not have minded.) And yes, I paid for Mark and Alyssa's tickets. Don't throw me that side-eye. You'd have a better chance of escaping Tribeca with your bone marrow intact than getting any comps out of Kathy during the Broadway run. Not that I blame her. People think performing artists have tons of free seats to hand out, like sandwich coupons or hand jobs. But the reality is, especially in a relatively intimate theater like the Belasco, with the high overhead that comes with any Broadway production—even just a stool and a microphone—every dollar matters.

Halfway through the run we had our routine down to a science. I would show up at the hotel each afternoon with chicken fingers from my favorite pub in the West Village and wash them down with a can of Diet Sunkist while Kathy had her hair and makeup done. What? That's not a typical meal for a Broadway gay? You'll be even more appalled to learn that after the first couple shows, Kathy's publicist Whitney and I started sneaking out around the corner to Planet Hollywood for more chicken fingers while Kathy was onstage. For me, the chicken fingers at Planet Hollywood are a culinary dependence, one so bizarre it almost qualifies as a fetish. I suppose if I were ever to attend a meeting of Overeaters Anonymous I would have to get up and say, "My name is Jack and I'm hooked on the chicken fingers at Planet Hollywood." I know, I know, Planet Hollywood, it's where culture goes to give up. Just looking up at the sign makes my soul dry-heave. But, here's the deal: they bread the chicken fingers in Cap'n Crunch cereal. Yeah. Take a moment to absorb how incredible that is, because once you do, you're going to be checking yourself and a platter of that shit into the nearest hourly motel.

We'd rush back with several takeout orders, and dive into them with Kathy's assistant Tiffany. Kathy would finish up and come back to the dressing room. "What did you think?" she'd ask, thinking we'd watched every minute of her performance. "You killed," I'd say, wiping crumbs off my shirt.

One night after the show we dined at Orso on West 46th Street with the legendary Gloria Vanderbilt, who happens to be the mother of my boss, Anderson Cooper. Kathy and Gloria had become good friends since Anderson introduced them after our New Year's Eve show several years back. Gloria started calling Kathy her "fantasy daughter." They're adorable together, especially when they're talking about their vaginal lining, which is often. I, of course, was in gay heaven just to be included. Ms. Vanderbilt, as I called her the first few times we met, was everything: stylish, intelligent, more than a bit naughty, and still a force to be reckoned with at age eighty-six.

One night, months later, Gloria invited Kathy and me to a dinner party at her apartment. I was terrified I would make a gaffe. At one point I reached into a dish of brightly colored gummy bears for a little snack, which would have been delicious had they been gummy bears and not colorful crystal ornaments. Oh well. As long as I didn't sneeze on Gloria or blurt out factoids from her memoir during the salad course, "What was Marlon Brando like in bed?!"

I've never quite understood the fascination with Brando as a sexual being. I think of him as mumbly old Don Corleone in *The Godfather* and then as the real-life recluse who wandered around his Mulholland Drive compound without pants on, grunting and lobbing grapefruit at fans gathered on the other side of his gate. As much as I wanted to get to the bottom of his long-ago sex appeal, I just couldn't dare broach what that ingenious nutbag might have done with the graceful Gloria Vanderbilt. Not that the whole thing is a secret. Anderson and Gloria have each alluded to her acquaintance with Brando, indeed many of her love affairs, in their own books and on television. She even once referred to a lover as "the Nijinsky of cunnilingus." Ms. Vanderbilt, it turns out, knows a thing or two about a thing or two.

When it comes to men, Kathy is hardly a neophyte, but she's

not in Gloria's "Nijinsky of cunnilingus" category either. I know during that particular spring she would have been happy just to have met the Lawrence Welk of cunnilingus. What she does know a thing or two about, however, is doughnuts. Warm, fresh doughnuts, right out of the fry machine. We were driving in Los Angeles late one night when she pulled into a doughnut-shop parking lot. "Get out," she said. "We're getting doughnuts and you're driving home." I thought she was kidding, but ten minutes later she was fellating a cruller in the passenger seat while I white-knuckled the steering wheel of her Maserati, a car worth more than my CNN life insurance would have paid out if I died driving it.

Kathy is, in fact, such a doughnut aficionado that she will tell you, if you're a New Yorker, or even if you're not, about a place called the Donut Pub on West 14th Street and Seventh Avenue. Not only do they cook their own doughnuts right there in the shop, they're open twenty-four hours a day. Perfect for the carbohydrate-addicted insomniac, a label we both wore with pride and shame during her Broadway run.

I lost count of how many times I walked into the Donut Pub at 3:30 A.M. with Kathy Griffin. If there were a support group for dead-of-night doughnut binge eaters, we'd be charter members. In our defense, we never set out to have such gluttonous nights. The way it usually worked was: Kathy would take a taxi to my apartment on the Upper West Side and we would walk the seventy-something blocks down to the Donut Pub, en route to her hotel. It's an insane walk for any New Yorker to do, day or night, especially in the predawn hours when no one is up to any good. But, she's a voracious walker, that Kathy Griffin. I once made the mistake of trying to keep up with her on a hike in the Hollywood Hills. I lagged so far behind that at one point I flagged down a man on a bicycle and pleaded with him to carry a message to her, wherever she was (she was already home in the pool).

At least in New York we were on flat ground, so I had a chance. The walks give me the opportunity to get some exercise and chat with my friend. Kathy was less interested in the exercise and more interested in spotting homeless couples and pointing out that they'd found love and I was going to bed alone. (At the 2011 Emmys, while Peter Dinklage, a little person, accepted his award for Best Supporting Actor in a Drama Series and thanked his beautiful girlfriend, Kathy leaned over and said to me, "I'd just like to point out that Dinklage is getting laid tonight and you're not.") It's not that she thought I was unlovable, per se, she just thought I was a hopeless slob. One night I made the mistake of having her over to my apartment. I hadn't cleaned as well as I should have. There may have been a cockroach on the floor and an empty box or seven of Cocoa Krispies on my counter. Kathy kept muttering about calling a crew from the TV show *Hoarders*. When I die, I want my surviving loved ones (my sister and my dog) to fill my casket with Cocoa Krispies. In death as in life. And have my wake at the Donut Pub.

The week on Broadway went by fast. Ten shows in eight days. Kathy sold more than a million dollars' worth of tickets and received a standing ovation every night. Her comedic mentor Joan Rivers came backstage to congratulate her. She was profiled on ABC's *Nightline* and got a great review in the *New York Times*. And while she didn't end up getting a Tony—they eliminated the "special event" category—it was a high point and I was proud to be a few steps behind her, holding her purse and what remained of the chocolate leg with my mangled hand. On closing night I rushed over to the Belasco from the GLAAD Media Awards at the Marriott Marquis to greet Kathy as she stepped offstage for the final time. She looked at me with a mixture of joy and disgust. We had dinner reservations, and I had crumbs on my shirt.

Mmmmm CHEESE

The first time I saw Peter Jennings in person, he was smoking a cigarette. I would only recall that detail as significant years later, after he was diagnosed with lung cancer. As he did with nearly everything, he made the inhalation of carbon monoxide look debonair. Though, if any impressionable youths are reading, remember the key term is not "debonair," but "lung cancer." It was January of the year 2000 and Mr. Jennings was at the University of New Hampshire, where I was a student, to moderate a Democratic presidential primary debate. A firm believer that celebrities are no different than the rest of us, I thought nothing of going up to him and introducing myself as an aspiring television journalist. I'm lying. I did a commando roll behind a concrete pillar and watched him from afar.

I encountered Mr. Jennings again later that same day, this

time indoors minus his cigarette. (I like to think he smoked Dunhills from the U.K., purposely leaving the trashier Marlboro Lights for Ted Koppel.) This time, I felt comfortable enough to say hello. After a kind and gracious few minutes of conversation, he wished me well in my pursuit of journalistic success and declined my offer to bear his children.

Growing up in the 1980s and 1990s, there was no one in whose footsteps I wanted to follow more than Peter Jennings. (Sorry to disappoint you, Dad.) He, Tom Brokaw, and Dan Rather were the three most important broadcasters in the United States. I wanted to be them . . . any of them, it didn't matter which one. Well, maybe a little less so Dan Rather because he's, you know, nuts.

That dream is long since dashed. Peter Jennings is dead, Tom Brokaw retired to Montana to count his money, and Dan Rather is the guy in Central Park who shouts at squirrels. There is no longer the voice-of-God anchorman. And, perhaps, that's as it should be. I still enjoy the 6:30 P.M. network news. Minus commercials, you get twenty-two minutes of much of what you need to know. As for what to do with the remaining time, well, as far as I'm concerned, nothing ushers in an episode of *Wheel of Fortune* quite like eight minutes of fellatio.

There's no disputing that more Americans are getting their news from other sources—cable television, the Internet, and, of course, Jon Stewart. Every day I hear the same thing. "You guys should be more like Jon Stewart. You know who's great? Jon Stewart. You should watch Jon Stewart. Jon Stewart, Jon Stewart, Jon Stewart." You know what? Shut the fuck up. I hear you. Jon Stewart is smart and hilarious. He's going to find a cure for cancer, and he's hung like a horse. I. HEAR. YOU.

I've never asked Jon Stewart about this notion that somehow he is Generation Y's answer to Peter Jennings. I've never met him. I suppose I could, not because he knows who I am or would care to learn I exist, but because it would not be unprecedented for me to throw the name of one Anderson Cooper around to obtain a celebrity meet-and-greet. Though, I'm careful never to use Anderson's influence in an unethical manner. It's not like I make hard-to-get dinner reservations under his name and then, upon arrival, tell the maitre d' that he was too drunk to make it. And I certainly don't introduce myself at bars by saying, "Hi, I'm Anderson Cooper. This is what I look like without my wig."

If I do ever meet Jon Stewart, I'll perhaps ask him about the people who go around bragging at cocktail parties that they don't need to watch anything besides his show to stay informed. Often these people will announce that not only do they only watch *The Daily Show,* they only watch it online, because they don't own a TV. There's a name for these people. They're called assholes.

What Stewart does so well—better than anyone—is call out people who are full of shit. So when I hear someone boasting they're up to speed on urgent issues of global consequence and *"only* watch *The Daily Show,"* I know they're full of shit. That's like getting all your comedy from Lesley Stahl. By all means, watch *The Daily Show.* It's genius, but would it kill you to also watch *60 Minutes,* or at least sleep with someone who does? I've seen Jon Stewart interviewed when he's been asked about people who consider him to be America's most respected newsman, and he always says that he is first and foremost a comedian, and that maybe if the news media did their jobs better, they might be more respected, a valid point.

I don't know Bill Maher, but I like him. I had dinner with him one night in November 2010. I was at Larry King's house, loitering around some emergency finger food. Kathy Griffin approached me and asked if I'd like to leave and go out to dinner with her, Bill, and his girlfriend. It took me all of a second to say yes, and that was before I knew that the dinner tab was being footed by another party guest, *Ocean's Eleven* producer Jerry Weintraub. He had insisted on sending us to his favorite restaurant in West Hollywood, Il Piccolino. OK, Jerry Weintraub, if you say so. Done and done. There's something about ordering food when a person you don't know has called ahead to pay. The words "lobster cocktail" come out so much easier.

It wasn't the meal that stays with me from that night, though everything tastes better when someone else is paying. Nor was it anything Bill Maher said, though he made many interesting and hilarious points. It was that he was a good listener. He didn't have to pay attention to anything I had to say. He didn't have to consider any of my ideas, but he did. That's my kind of thinker and, for that matter, my kind of celebrity. It's also easy to fall under the Bill Maher spell when you realize he knows Warren Beatty. Whatever world that is, I want in. I'll die a happy man if I live a life half as cool as the life of Warren Beatty. Hell, I'll settle for a life half as cool as Warren Beatty's jawline.

Maher, Stewart, and Stephen Colbert. They are the Brokaw, Jennings, and Rather of my generation. And with each election cycle the three of them become more relevant and influential. Which is a great thing. And it has not gone unnoticed by other television shows. News executives worship Jon Stewart. If I got paid based on how many times I heard someone say, "We need a guest who's witty, pull-no-punches, a Jon Stewart type," I'd have long since retired to a bathtub full of tapioca pudding. And, yes, that's how I envision my golden years.

What I've always found so bizarre is how certain members of the media don't comprehend how most nights Stewart, Colbert, and Maher are saying, "You guys are ass-clowns and you're dumbing down the country." It's as if the television news industry doesn't realize that *The Daily Show* is laughing at it, not with it. News organizations' interpretation of that criticism is along the lines of "OMG, LOL, good one, guys. We love you, too."

I think many of us who make a living in journalism are envious of Stewart, Colbert, and Maher. I know I am. Unlike traditional news programming, they're free to call out grotesque carnival barkers on the national scene and say, "No, this is wrong, this is ludicrous, you people should be in restraints." Sometimes I feel like I'm screaming on the inside, like I'm going to explode, listening to some of the people we in the media put on the air. I was once reprimanded for tweeting that the media should not treat Donald Trump as a serious person. I appreciate that fairness and objectivity are the basic journalistic principles that have guided our profession for decades, but Edward R. Murrow did not live in an era of real-time insanity.

In case you haven't noticed—blogs, YouTube, Twitter, Facebook—the world has turned into a giant bucket of crazy. Yes, we can go on as if all news should be presented the way Walter Cronkite did it, but things have changed. The line between the fringe and the mainstream has become blurred to the point that I'm not sure one still exists.

Of course, there are plenty of journalists who don't suffer fools. One such is Anderson Cooper. And I'm not just saying that because, as I write this, he's staring at me, fiddling with a bottle of pepper spray. There was a night in 2010 when we were doing a segment about a ridiculous piece of legislation in Arizona that was being proposed in the wake of President Obama's birth certificate "controversy." Our guest was a state legislator who said, having seen President Obama's birth certificate on the Internet, he had no reason to doubt his citizenship. He was, however, voting for the bill—which would have required presidential candidates to present their birth certificates to the Arizona secretary of state—because, he said, with a wink-wink to the Obama-hating conspiracy theorists, "You can't believe everything you read on the Internet . . . I've never investigated it." Instead of giving an irrational person the benefit of the doubt, which—in my opinion—cable news does too often, Anderson said what every sane person was thinking at that moment, "The information is out there . . . it has been released, it has been shown. There are some people who don't believe it, but there are also some people who believe the moon is made out of cheese. And you can say you've never investigated it, but I think you would probably say the moon is not made out of cheese." Mmmmmm . . . cheese.

There is a huge difference between real, honest-to-goodness "news" and much of the cable news blathering satirized so skillfully by Jon Stewart and company. There is a journalistic tradition that has an important place in our world. And it's heartening that certain networks—CNN among them—continue to give so-called hard news priority. Not all the time. There are plenty of flashy visuals, gimmicks, and slogans. The problem is that hard news on cable television doesn't attract the number of viewers it once did. What a lot of people seem to like, according to the ratings, are the opinionated partisan shows that provide Jon Stewart so much fodder. But, a lot of people like crack, too. That doesn't mean they need it.

I write all this as if I'm not part of the problem. As if I spend my days producing documentaries on the plight of the homeless. Not quite. I'm proud of the work we do most nights, but I've also produced my share of screaming political pundits. I've even appeared on-air to discuss pop culture, arguably the least important news of the day. But, even pop culture has its place in the news cycle. Even if it didn't, I love putting on makeup.

For me to delve into media analysis and act as though I'm somehow above the echo chamber to which I contribute would be wrong. As if I'd rather watch a story on the economy than *Dancing with the Stars*. Trust me, I'll take Shannen Doherty doing the rumba over Tim Geithner any day.

I once read a quote from Phil Griffin, the head of MSNBC, who said he resented the notion that CNN does "the Lord's work." I'm not sure who put that notion out there into the ether, but I've never known anyone who felt that way. The idea that people viewed us as riding around on our cable news high horses made me cringe. I mean, yes, I do think I'm the second coming of Christ, but that has nothing to do with journalism. It has to do with my firm ass.

On the most basic level, it's the people who take themselves too seriously, who have no sense of self-awareness, who bother me. Yes, journalism is a noble profession. Without a doubt. And there are anchors, correspondents, producers, photojournalists, and other crew members who risk their lives to bring the world important stories from places of great danger and suffering. And there are countless hardworking people in newsrooms and studios. But let's not pretend that there isn't also a lot of over-the-top crap on cable news. The immodesty and lack of perspective are staggering.

Jon Stewart, Bill Maher, and Stephen Colbert pick up on that lack of modesty. No wonder Stewart, in particular, eviscerates the various cable networks night after night. Life is too short to lose sleep over the future of cable news. Either way, I don't have time to think about it now. It's almost time to watch *The Daily Show*.

AS THE **BALL DROPS**

I once filled out an online dating profile that asked, "What is the most embarrassing thing that you're willing to admit about yourself?" I wrote, "I've been to both Olive Gardens in Manhattan." In New York, dining at a chain restaurant is tantamount to buying your underwear at CVS, which, incidentally, I also do. I love the Olive Garden, and not just because the breadsticks are warm and look like dildos. They also make great spaghetti with meat sauce. I'd been going to the OG, as the regulars call it, in Times Square for years, starting long before I moved to the city. Whenever I would come to New York for a visit, my first meal would always be there. Even then my friends would snicker at me, though that was nothing compared to the grief I got when I continued my patronage after becoming a New York resident.

"Who the hell goes to the Olive Garden in Times Square?" my friend Kirk would ask.

"Me and a bunch of Belgian tourists, what's it to you?" I'd say.

Rarely can I get anyone to eat with me at that location. My friend Mark doesn't mind the one in Chelsea, though he ducks into the door like he's entering a tiramisu-serving whorehouse.

I know how ridiculous it is in a city like New York, with thousands of restaurants to choose from, to go to chain establishments. I'm not proud of it. I don't want to know what it says about me when I stumbled into a cab drunk, alone, at 5 P.M. on a Sunday no less, that I directed the driver to take me to Planet Hollywood. For added measure, I said, "Step on it." It was bad enough I was going to a restaurant conceived by Bruce Willis—I didn't need to start talking like him. I tell myself that I'm just taking comfort food to a new level. While normal people go to the kitchen and open up a box of macaroni and cheese, I throw on some sweatpants and take the subway to the gates of hell.

That's a key problem. As much as I enjoy the food I get there, I can't stand Times Square. It's packed with people who don't know where they're going and stop every five feet to take photographs of giant M&M's and billboards of Taylor Swift. So in late 2008, when asked if I wanted to be the on-site producer for CNN's *New Year's Eve Live* with Anderson Cooper and Kathy Griffin, I was hesitant. Part of me thought it would be a fun experience. Another part of me thought spending New Year's Eve amongst a million people wearing dumb hats and penned in like cattle was something even a fistful of Xanax couldn't handle. I said yes, because I loved Anderson and Kathy, and also, to be honest, because I didn't have anything better to do. I wanted to be the guy with the steady date at the subtly stylish party in Tribeca filled with sexy guests, where someone is smoking pot in the bathroom and Ryan Seacrest is mocked by the occasional hipster who glances at the muted TV broadcast of ABC's New Year's Rockin' Eve. But to be invited to partake in such an evening, one must be socially well adjusted.

I guess it's just tough to get behind a night that's supposed to climax with a midnight kiss. That magical moment never seems to materialize. I don't know why. I try to be charming, and I even have that uplifting little toast, "Here's to another year down the drain."

That first year, I didn't know what I was doing. My primary responsibility was to make sure Anderson got into Times Square safely and on schedule. Colleagues of mine, who knew what they were doing, informed me that security guards would be picking us up from CNN headquarters to drive us the approximately ten to fifteen blocks to our staging area. Anderson, of course, just wanted to walk down there like a regular New Yorker, but I concocted some story about how that would be a logistical problem and the security guards had special passes to drop us where we needed to be, which was true, though I was lazy and just didn't want to walk.

Anderson was mortified as soon as we walked out of the Time Warner Center. The security guards' SUV was not only outfitted with flashing lights and a siren, but also appeared armored. He gave me a look that said I was a dead man. Naturally I couldn't hop in fast enough, eager to blow through some red lights on the company dime. I sat in the wrong seat, though, and the head guard told me to move. Anderson had to sit there. There's a special seat for the protectee. I should have known that, having seen *Guarding Tess* with Nicolas Cage and Shirley MacLaine.

I was kicked to the rear of the SUV, with the machine guns or the groceries or whatever they had back there. Once we got to Times Square, through all the barricades and checkpoints, our security team gave us our cheerful New Year's Eve instructions: "If anything happens, like a dirty bomb goes off, wait for us, we'll come get you." Yeah, well you know what? If something happens—and by the way, thanks for mentioning that possibility—I'll be running for my life up Broadway, with a stop at Carnegie Deli to loot cheesecake, time permitting.

Walking through Times Square with Anderson Cooper on New Year's Eve is what I imagine walking around with Elvis was like, except Anderson isn't quite as sweaty. Everyone freaks out and screams. They've all got novelty eyeglasses in the shape of 2012 or whatever year we're approaching. I don't even think they're allowed to leave their livestock pens to use the bathroom, so I just assume most of them are covered in their own frozen urine. Oh right, that's the other thing. It's usually freezing that night. Good times.

I always get us there ahead of schedule. I go by my grandparents' motto that unless you're an hour early, you're late. But, of course, Anderson never wants to wait inside the warm satellite truck, he likes to hang outside, chatting with the crew and greeting revelers. So, because he's so selfish, I have to stand outside, too, shivering and stuffing hand warmers in places they weren't meant to be. Anderson and I may have arrived in Times Square early that first year, but Kathy sure didn't. I remember being up on the riser, just a few minutes before we were scheduled to go on the air, wondering where the hell she was. She showed up with moments to spare, shouting about taping an audio wire to her wig. It was a close call that would turn out to be the least of our problems that night. The first sign of trouble was when she started throwing things at the Jonas Brothers. They were performing on Seacrest's show. She also punched Anderson in the stomach a few times, just for fun. When they introduced musical guest Lil' Wayne, he replied by thanking "Anderson Cooper and Miss Kathy Griffin Lee." Lil' Wayne—who had a team of pole dancers whose moves were so suggestive that CNN cut away during the live show and blurred them out from future broadcasts—thought she was Kathie Lee Gifford.

That was nothing compared to the moment that would go down in New Year's Eve—and YouTube—history. At one point near the end of the show, as Anderson was getting ready to go to commercial, the crowd started getting rowdy on the street below our platform. The ball had dropped and the police had taken down the barricades. People were drawn to the TV platform like moths to a light. And, of course, they started shouting and being obnoxious, until Kathy let them have it, "Shut up! You know what, screw you, I'm working . . . I don't go to your job and knock the dicks out of your mouth!"

It was one of those moments that I'll never forget. She immediately asked if we'd still been on the air. I confirmed with the control room that indeed we had. After that was a haze. No one remembers anything else from that night. No one recalls that the show that year also featured a performance from a musician who, at that point, was still unknown to many people. I wonder what ever happened to that Lady Gaga.

"Jesus Fucking Christ, where's the fire, Mary?" the voice asked as soon as I answered the phone. It was December 2009 and Kathy Griffin was calling because I'd been pestering her people—Team Griffin—for details on what she wanted to talk about with Anderson on New Year's Eve. Amazingly she was back after Dickmouthgate, though not without an ironclad contract. It stipulated that if she cursed on-air she would forfeit her salary. Unsurprisingly, she informed me that the contract would be her primary topic for the show. She even forwarded me some letters from her attorney that she wanted printed out, so she could read them on the air. She also asked if we would be broadcasting from the same location, in her words, "that cheap-ass, rickety platform next to the dude from Telemundo." I told her that we would be and that one segment idea we'd come up with was for Anderson to show her photos of celebrities and newsmakers, kind of a free association exerise. Fine, she said. We didn't talk more about it. I knew by then that Kathy and Anderson were smart enough just to do their thing. That's when the show is best, when they're just riffing off each other. And when she's punching him.

The executive producer wanted Anderson to hold up the celebrity photos on the riser, like a pop culture Rorschach test. The pictures needed to be big enough and of suitable quality to be visible on television. You'd think that a media giant of CNN's size and stature would have the capability to print out photos. You'd be wrong. I went to Kinko's.

We made it to the big night. Anderson, Kathy, Team Griffin,

and I all gathered on the riser, just before showtime. Kathy itched to get started. She couldn't wait to tease Anderson and CNN about her contract. She'd even brought along her checkbook, in case she slipped up and had to give the money back. It was actually my checkbook, which she'd ordered me to turn over to her the previous night, when she appeared on *Anderson Cooper 360* and grilled our pregnant news anchor, Erica Hill, on what she was going to do with her placenta.

The show began. Everything was going fine. Anderson and Kathy had their usual great chemistry. I was trying to warm my hands in between my legs. We were all a bit frightened by Jennifer Lopez "singing" on the platform behind us in some sort of gold mesh leotard, but we managed to keep our show on track. Until we got to those fucking flash cards. Anderson held up a photo of the infamous "Balloon Boy," the Colorado kid whose father briefly scammed the world into believing that his son was trapped in a giant Jiffy Pop container soaring high above Colorado. Anyway, Balloon Boy's real name is Falcon Heene. By that point, twenty minutes into the show, Kathy was going right up to the line with every word that sounded like a curse. "Falcon? Fuckin? Falcon? How do you say it?" she asked. Yeah, she slipped up, though it was barely distinguishable. None of us on the platform realized she'd said it, nor had anyone back in the control room. But a reporter from the *New York Times* called our publicist. Our people checked the tape. Yes, she had baited everyone into catching her in a slipup and she had slipped up. At least, after all those years of sitting at home doing nothing, I finally had a New Year's tradition.

Kathy and I grew much tighter over the years, so tight that I'd even seen her "bangin' bikini bod" in real life. One afternoon we were hanging out at her friend Gloria Estefan's house on Star Island, just off Miami Beach, when Kathy saw a cruise ship pass by. Like any normal person would do, she ran out onto Gloria's dock and ripped off her bikini top and flashed the passengers. Unbeknownst to us, there were paparazzi hiding in the vicinity. They got several shots of her topless, waving her arms in the air. In one photograph I can be seen next to her; I am in an awkward stance and my facial expression is one of complete horror. The photo gave the impression that I was disgusted by Kathy's boobs, which, by the way, I was not. I had tripped running onto the dock, thus my expression. That story, however, did not make its way to Conan O'Brien. When Kathy was next on his show, Conan put the photo on-screen and then re-created my expression. I had messages the next morning from friends confused about how I was spending my free time. As much as I had gotten used to the paparazzi when I was around Kathy or Anderson, the experience of being surreptitiously photographed from a great distance was new. I was much more accustomed to the photographers being in close range and saying to me, "Excuse me, sir, can you step out of the shot? Sir, your elbow is still in the picture."

It's never my decision whether or not Kathy is invited back to cohost New Year's Eve, but I always put in a good word. I was relieved to hear that CNN executives wanted her to help the network usher in 2011. We gathered that year in Times Square an hour before showtime, at which point I started badgering Anderson, unsuccessfully, to buy me breadsticks at the Olive Garden. Apparently he had more important things to do.

Kathy arrived early that year because I dispatched a security car with lights and a siren to fetch her. She dragged Anderson through the throngs of people, searching for Ryan Seacrest. She was a woman on a mission. What she was going to do if she found him, no one knew, but it would have required the intervention of the mounted police. Though they didn't find Seacrest (and a police officer told them that they never would because he's too short), Kathy did manage to crash Carson Daly's show—live—on NBC.

It went without saying that it was in everyone's best interests if there wasn't another slipup on our broadcast. I went so far as to print out a NO SWEARING sign that I kept pointed in Kathy's direction through much of the night. I had a few cameos of my own that year. At one point, when Anderson and Kathy were talking about Twitter, Anderson plugged my page and pulled me by the scruff of the neck in front of the camera. And later, four minutes before midnight, Kathy pulled me on camera for a big wet kiss. It'd been a long time since I kissed a lady on the mouth, much less on worldwide television. But it was everything I like in a smooch: impromptu and minty.

The New Year arrived with nary a curse from Kathy Griffin's Altoids-flavored lips. We were all relieved. Anderson, Kathy, her assistant Tiffany, and I repaired to Kathy's hotel suite for our own little sad but wonderful after-party. Anderson was lying on the floor because his back was bothering him, Kathy was taking off her wig (or "magic hair" as she calls it), and Tiffany and I were eating cookies and giggling. It was already a perfect start to

2011, and that was before Kathy decided she wanted doughnuts at 4 A.M.

It's around five o'clock on an autumn evening and I'm aboard a private jet descending into Albany, New York. I'm along as a guest of Kathy. She is performing in a couple of hours at the Palace Theatre. There are three of us in her entourage that night: Tiffany, Tiffany's friend Janine, and I. We debate where we should get dinner. I pull out my iPhone and search for the nearest Olive Garden. The mocking is instantaneous. When I protest, I'm informed that I should just be glad I wasn't thrown off the plane in midair for suggesting such a ridiculous option. The argument turns out to be moot. The restaurant is out of the way. We skip dinner, making do with Junior Mints and Reese's Peanut Butter Cups backstage. On the flight back to New York City, we revisit the topic of a meal. I challenge the group to come up with something that sounds better than a basket of breadsticks at the Times Square Olive Garden. They ask me if I've been taking my medication.

Three weeks later, my first trip to Las Vegas is coming to a close. I say goodbye to Kathy, Tiffany, and other friends as they climb into the limousine headed for the airport to return to Los Angeles.

"What are you going to do until your flight leaves?" Kathy asks.

"Oh, I'll figure something out. I'll probably just get lunch and then go see a movie." I've been waiting all weekend to get to the local Olive Garden. I've already looked it up. It's not on the Strip; it's somewhere out in the desert. I hail a cab in front of Caesars Palace and give the driver an address. He looks at me quizzically, even more so when I explain, "It's the Olive Garden." Driving out there, I feel like I'm in a scene from *Casino*. Maybe this is how it ends. Me in an Olive Garden on the outskirts of Vegas. If not, I'll at least have something to add to my online dating profile.

MR. PIT STAINS
GOES TO WASHINGTON

The fact that the "bus station" was the curb outside the Sbarro on Seventh Avenue probably should have been an indication that my fellow passengers and I would not be getting stellar service. Yet, I was still caught off guard when the bus pulled up—thirty minutes late—and the driver started yelling at us. Nice to meet you, too, buddy. For all the times I'd been screamed at outside the Seventh Avenue Sbarro—and who hasn't been?—I'd never encountered someone so unpleasant or hostile to luggage. "If y'all don't back the hell up *right now*, I'm going to get behind that wheel and leave your asses here," he said. As we pulled away from the curb, en route to Washington, D.C., I looked toward the front of the bus, where the driver was leaning on the horn. It was probably too late to ask to see his credentials.

It was an unusual trip for me to be going on. I was paying

for my own hotel room, which, as the CNN accountants will attest, is something to which I'm opposed. That's why I was traveling by bus instead of by train or plane. My weekend in Washington didn't qualify as official business and my room service bill sure as hell wasn't going to take care of itself. I was also traveling alone. Granted, I'm a regular at the singles' table when it comes to weddings or holiday parties or my own birthday, but this was a weekend when everyone was being seen for the sake of being seen. I'm above that, or at least pretend I am. But I should have brought a date.

When people say they would never be caught dead at a certain high-profile party, it just means they weren't invited. Which is why I'm always saying, "Oh, I wouldn't be caught dead there." Somewhere along the line there was obviously a mix-up. I got put on the annual guest list for a famous brunch thrown during the weekend of the White House Correspondents' Association Dinner. The dinner itself is the main event and I wouldn't be going to that. Thanks for nothing, Wolf Blitzer.

Even if I wouldn't be attending the black-tie gala, I was excited to be going to the "garden chic" brunch, which was more my style anyway. Except for the chic part. The bus ride was mostly calm, save for the occasional expletive coming from the driver. He dumped us off in a parking lot at Union Station, where I went in search of an ATM. As luck would have it, the only one I could find was in use by a woman who—about two seconds after I took my place in line—turned around and lost her shit. *"PLEASE stand back,"* she shouted.

"Excuse me?" I said, not having a clue what she was talking about, as I was at least ten feet away.

"Are you going to stand back or not? I would like some goddamn

space, SIR," she continued. I was half-tempted to set her up on a date with my bus driver but figured she probably had to get back to her job, which I presumed was congresswoman.

Maybe it was naïve of me to think things would get better outside at the taxi stand. I walked over to where a driver was leaning against his cab. I told him where I needed to go and—silly me—I assumed I'd get in the car and he'd take me there. But apparently Washington, D.C., works on some sort of third-world bartering system. The driver started to walk along the curb, asking *other people* if they needed to go in the general direction he was taking me. When I asked what was going on, he just pointed to a placard inside the backseat of the taxi, which went into detail about how D.C. law required passengers to share cabs whenever possible. I don't remember what the reason was, probably something Ed Begley, Jr., cooked up about saving the planet from fossil fuel emissions. By the way, I totally support that law, unless it means sharing a cab with a stranger. All I could picture was the door opening and the woman from the ATM getting in.

The draw of White House Correspondents' Association weekend is that it's a bizarre mix of political power brokers, Hollywood stars, and starstruck journalists. Truthfully, it's an insufferable mix. But it was my first time being invited down there and I won't pretend like I wasn't initially dazzled. The way it works is that news organizations compete to see who can bring the most high-profile guests. Some people you hear about beforehand, others are last-minute surprises. That year, as I walked into the brunch, people were giggling and pointing at three guys in front of me. They turned out to be the Jonas Brothers. I kind of felt bad for them. When I saw them later, they appeared to be having as much fun as you'd expect from virgins at a garden party.

I was sweating. It must have been 90 degrees underneath that tent. And the hotter it got, the more confused I became about everyone mingling around me. On one side of me was President Obama's senior adviser, David Axelrod, and on the other side of me was Matthew Morrison from *Glee*. It was like one of those weddings where the bride and groom's families have nothing in common. Which, of course, are the best weddings. Except here no one was having sex in a linen closet.

I decided to just hang out near my CNN power-trio colleagues: John King, Dana Bash, and Ed Henry. They were so sweet when they saw me. They were like, "Hey, what the hell are you doing—um, I mean, great to see you." It seemed as if every few minutes they mysteriously grew further away from me, but I just chalked that up to the heat.

Meanwhile, I was fixated on the woman sitting with Greta Van Susteren. She looked familiar, but I couldn't think of her name. I knew she was someone famous. Finally I asked someone. "That's Kim Kardashian" was the horrified reply, as if I'd just asked who was on the one-dollar bill. OK, fine, I should have been able to identify Kim Kardashian. My logic is that I'd spent so much energy judging her, I'd never bothered to learn what she looked like. I hadn't even seen her sex tape, a piece of Americana so storied that I think it has its own question on the U.S. citizenship test.

It's easy to make fun of Kim Kardashian when you see her somewhere like Washington, or, you know, anywhere. But I kind of relish what she brings to a weekend like that. Yes, I roll my eyes at the spectacle of D.C. elites kissing up to random celebrities. It's embarrassing. But it's hardly the most obnoxious thing that goes on in Washington each year. Have you ever heard some of the things that come out of the mouths of our elected representatives? There are comments far more troublesome than "What's Bruce Jenner like as a stepdad?" And the brunch itself helps raise money to support finding a cure for epilepsy, so if trotting out Chace Crawford every year helps with that, I'm all for it. And if that noble cause just happens to provide me with an opportunity to quiz him on *Gossip Girl* plotlines, so much the better.

Mostly, though, I kept to myself. I didn't have the nerve to go up to Chevy Chase. I would have just started quoting lines from *Fletch* until he had security remove me. Nor did I approach Rupert Murdoch. I probably would have slipped into my Crocodile Dundee imitation.

I left the party with pit stains under my arms and pockets stuffed with finger foods. I may have become blasé about meeting political heavyweights and TV stars, but part of me was still the kid who instead of doing my homework listened intently as my dad talked about politics and watched the news. To walk in that swirl, even just as a no-name in a crowd of hundreds at that party, was something I never thought I'd experience. My dad would have loved that party. I would have called to tell him all about it, if not for the fact that by the time I left I was way too important.

Being in Washington, D.C., for White House Correspondents' Association weekend but not going to the actual dinner leaves a bit of a gap on one's schedule in the evening, before all the after-parties. As it happened, I had a friend hospitalized with a brain aneurysm. Fortunately, by the time I got there, I knew that Chris Licht, then the executive producer of MSNBC's *Morning Joe* and husband of my dear friend Jenny Blanco, was going to be OK. I was comfortable greeting him in his room at George Washington University Hospital with, "Shit, you'll do anything to be the center of attention, huh?" NBC had sent him an iPad to help pass the time, which I snatched from his hands. If you ever want to steal electronics from someone, I suggest an intensive care patient attached to wires.

Chris, Jenny, and I were hanging out in his room for a while when Joe Scarborough and Mika Brzezinski stopped by on their way to the dinner. There's something fun about rummaging through a gift basket that doesn't belong to you while people in formal wear give themselves a once-over in a hospital mirror. It was like watching two people go to the prom, except instead of high school kids posing for photos with parents in a living room, there were two morning-show hosts posing with their producer in a hospital bed. Mika damn near climbed in there with him. I was worried she was going to dislodge his pee tube.

I went back to my hotel and got ready for the after-party, which entailed brushing the crumbs off my khakis. Khakis, by the way, apparently aren't the best thing to wear to a party being thrown after a black-tie dinner. Neither is a blue blazer or pink shirt. I looked as though I was about to push off from the dock for a sail around Nantucket. As I tend to do when I'm alone, or with others, I hovered around the dessert table. I didn't know who was paying for all that chocolate, but I was determined to eat as much as I could before they stopped me. I came up for air to talk to some CNN colleagues, none of whom complimented me on my outfit. Making the rounds at the venue, I realized I was as much out of my element at the after-party as I had been at the brunch. I didn't belong there. I didn't fit in. I hardly knew anyone. But then I saw Kim Kardashian arrive and that made me feel better.

She didn't know many people there, either.

that all of the celebrity presenters were fair game in terms of approachability, except one: "Do not talk to Demi Moore" was the word from the event planners. Where was a hero when I needed one?

Officially, my assignment was to hang out backstage with Anderson Cooper and post Twitter updates about all the excitement, like brushing lint off his jacket and pretending not to stare at Halle Berry. But there was something about being sandwiched in between movie stars and everyday people being honored for changing the world. My self-esteem dropped to about zero, and I soon abandoned Anderson in favor of sitting in a dark corner eating brown sugar Pop-Tarts. I tried to distract myself by looking at Bon Jovi's feathered bangs but, still, I kept one eye out for Demi Moore. At one point I heard a big commotion around the corner. When I asked someone what happened, I was told, "Demi Moore just walked by." I took out another Pop-Tart and used it to dab the tears from my eyes. Then I ate it.

The thing about awards shows and celebrities is that those kinds of "do-not-talk-to-her" edicts rarely, if ever, come from the stars themselves. They come from overprotective handlers who, in fairness, get paid to keep events like that as hassle-free as possible for their clients. But I wasn't just some garden-variety Demi Moore fan. First, I could quote every line from *Indecent Proposal.* Which is not at all creepy. Second, she and I have a mutual friend, and the same literary agent. We're practically blood relatives. As luck would have it, I had received an e-mail from that mutual friend, Soleil Moon Frye, who asked me how the event was going. Great, I replied, except, so far, no Demi. Soleil said I should absolutely go say hello and, not only that, she would text

HOLLYWOOD HOLIDAYS

There's a scene in the movie *Indecent Proposal* when Demi Moore is trying on a black dress in a Las Vegas boutique. Robert Redford, who is infatuated with her, watches from behind. She twists her hair atop her head and tilts her body ever so slightly while looking in a mirror. That was the moment I fell in love with Demi Moore, which I'm sure she'd be delighted to know. She represented everything I thought I wanted: a raspy sex appeal rooted in strength. I turned out to be more interested in a raspy sex appeal rooted in men's jeans, but my affection for Ms. Moore never waned.

So when I was asked to help out with the 2010 CNN Heroes gala in Los Angeles, where she was slated to be a presenter, I thought I might have the chance to meet her. Of course, when I heard the briefing on backstage protocol, we were told

Demi to give her a heads-up. Because that's how Punky Brewster rolls, America.

A few minutes later, I was sitting on my milk crate, trying to hide from Anderson, when Demi Moore entered the backstage area. Fuck it, I thought. This is my chance. There's always that split second when you meet a famous person; just as you go up to them, there's a look in their eyes that says "Please don't be a fucking lunatic." If Demi Moore had that look in her eyes, I didn't notice it. I was too busy noticing how stunning she was in person. I managed to stammer out, "Hi, we have a mutual friend, Soleil Moon Frye." Which, by the way, is an amazing way to begin a conversation. Ms. Moore was delightful, everything my teenage fantasy hoped she would be. Luckily, I said goodbye and walked away before I asked her if she still had that dress from *Indecent Proposal,* and, if so, could she try it on for me.

The CNN Heroes show taped that year in L.A. the weekend before Thanksgiving. Driving along Sunset Boulevard, stopping at In-N-Out Burger—I was lacking in incentives to hurry back east to spend the holiday with my family. So when Kathy Griffin invited me to stick around and spend Thanksgiving with her, I said yes. I enjoyed hanging out in L.A. with Kathy. I'd spent my thirtieth birthday with her a few months earlier. Not only did she welcome me and a group of my friends to her, as she describes it, "palatial mansion" for a night of Italian food, reality-TV watching, and cursing; she treated me to a birthday dinner at Chateau Marmont (Ricky Gervais stopped by our table because that's what happens when I agree to go somewhere other than the Olive Garden). Later that night Kathy took me to a pre-Emmys party as her guest. We drove there along Sunset Boulevard, in her Maserati, singing along to Patti LaBelle covers of Céline Dion songs. Occasionally, at red lights, she would lean out the window and shout at pedestrians, "Hey, everyone, look, it's me, Kathy Griffin!"

Kathy left the planning for what we'd do for Thanksgiving dinner up to me. At that point I had two invitations: one from Soleil and one from my friend Nia Vardalos, the hugely talented actress and writer behind *My Big Fat Greek Wedding*. I'd accepted Nia's offer first, which disappointed Soleil. And since hell hath no fury like Punky Brewster wielding a pumpkin pie full of "oh hell, no," I worked it out so Kathy and I would have dinner at Nia's and go to Soleil's for dessert.

Before Thanksgiving Day rolled around, Kathy and I had three nights to spend together at her aforementioned mansion. The first night I was there, so was ninety-year-old Maggie Griffin, famous to TV viewers for her scene-stealing appearances on *Kathy Griffin: My Life on the D-List*. Maggie didn't live at Kathy's house full-time, but she occasionally spent the night. Anyone who has ever watched the *D-List* knows that Mrs. Griffin has a fondness for wine of the boxed variety, which, upon my arrival, she whipped out in a much-appreciated gesture of hospitality. She and I discussed boxed wine's many upsides. According to Mrs. Griffin, it's easier for kids to open.

Sitting around the kitchen table, eating dinner and watching TV with Kathy and her mom was like a *D-List* episode except that there were no cameras around. Maggie kept giving Kathy unsolicited advice and asking her to change the channel to Fox News so she could watch her beloved Bill O'Reilly. In turn, Kathy threatened to cut off her mom's wine supply and told her to go do the dishes. Maggie and I, we were informed, would be "neighbors" in Kathy's home. Mrs. Griffin was assigned to the

Tuscany Suite and I was assigned to the nearby Princess Suite. I'm not joking.

Before Maggie could go to sleep, Kathy said, I needed to assist Maggie in putting on a new duvet cover. I don't know what happened to the previous duvet cover. I think Kathy just liked giving her mom tasks. Maggie and I tried to figure out which end of the cover went where and how to get the duvet into it, all the while presuming Kathy was right behind us, if not assisting at least supervising. Naturally, when we turned around, she was long gone, back upstairs watching *Bad Girls Club*. The duvet cover was a pain. Maggie and I struggled with it for a while before we realized it was the wrong size. Just then, I noticed Kathy's dogs, Larry and Pom Pom, were chewing something, in that way that dogs chew things they're not supposed to. I reached into their mouths and pulled out ketchup packets. Where do dogs get ketchup packets? Maggie carries a variety of items in her muumuu—just in case—including dried-out paper towels, plastic-wrapped pieces of hamburger, and, yes, ketchup packets. Because you just never know when you're going to need them.

I slept like a princess in the Princess Suite, despite Kathy telling me not to turn off the bank of security-camera monitors. "You want to see who is be coming to kill you," she advised. Lovely. I distracted myself by trying to learn how to signal SOS with the remote-controlled shades. I showered and dressed and went upstairs to find Kathy and Maggie sitting in the living room and drinking coffee. "Jake—Jake, did you hear me knocking on your door this morning?" Maggie asked. "I was going to see if you wanted me to make you pancakes." At which point Kathy choked on her coffee. "First of all," she told her mother, "his name is Jack, not Jake. Second, he didn't hear you because

he was fucking sleeping. And by the way, you haven't made pancakes in thirty years." I don't know what it's called when a gay
guy wants to marry his straight lady friend and her mother—
"twisted" is probably the word—all I know is I hadn't had that
much fun in a long time.

That first morning I was at Kathy's house I had to go put
in a day of work at the CNN Los Angeles bureau. As if depart-
ing for work from a gated estate weren't surreal enough, it felt
odd to be so well rested and energized by the warm Southern
California weather. I was used to getting three hours' sleep in
my loud and tiny New York apartment, waking up to Sammy's
breath. But it wasn't the mansion or the Maserati that made the
visit so special. The best part of staying with her was just she
and I, hanging out in our pajamas, shooting the shit, laughing it
up, and watching "Oprah's Favorite Things." By the end of my
visit I could recite everything that Oprah gave away, but mostly I
just walked around the mansion telling the dogs, "You're all getting iPaaaaaaaaaaaaaaaaaaads!"

After Oprah, we moved on to the rest of Kathy's DVR treasure trove, from the *Real Housewives* to *The Little Couple*. Apparently I was the only person in America unaware that TLC was
obsessed with shows about little people. *The Little Couple, The
Little Chocolatier*?! TLC has a borderline fetish. There's also a
show on Animal Planet about little people who rescue pit bulls.
That show makes me nervous.

Thanksgiving Day arrived. I woke up in the Princess Suite
and told myself that I was thankful for my health, my family, and my friends. Especially friends with remote-controlled
shades. By coincidence, my aunt and cousin were arriving
in Los Angeles that morning. I had no interest in getting out

of bed, much less putting on pants, but I knew I had to put in some family time. Kathy and I were due at Nia's house for Thanksgiving dinner at 4 P.M. I told her I was going to visit my aunt and cousin in Beverly Hills and that I'd be back by 3 P.M. All I would need was a half hour to shower and get dressed and then we could depart at 3:30.

"Don't be late," she warned.

"I won't be, don't worry," I said. "Do you need anything at the store?" We weren't quite an old married couple, but we were getting there.

I went over to Beverly Hills and picked up my aunt and cousin. Instead of just killing time by getting coffee, we decided that I'd give them a quick tour of some L.A. landmarks. When I pointed out the house where Michael Jackson died, my aunt nearly pulled the emergency break. She insisted on getting out and taking a picture in front of his gate. Every time we passed a big house my aunt would ask, "Who lives there?" So I did what any good tour guide would do: I just started making stuff up. "You see that house over there? That's where Lucille Ball lived." "Really?" my aunt said. "That looks like a church." "Well," I continued, "toward the end of her life the I Love Lucy residuals didn't pay too well and she had to live in the basement. By the way, that stucco mansion on the left, that's where Lassie mauled a Pomeranian."

They asked me what I was doing for Thanksgiving dinner, a question I had been dreading. "Well, Kathy and I are going over to Nia Vardalos's house," which of course made them lose their shit, not just because they wanted some star sightings but also because they're Greek. There was an awkward bit of silence before I asked, "So, what are you two doing for dinner?"

"Oh, nothing special," they said, "we'll probably just walk around and try to find an open restaurant." I knew what they were hoping for, that I would say, "Hey, I have an idea! Why don't you come with Kathy and me to Nia's house!" Well, that wasn't happening. I dropped them off and pointed them toward Denny's.

I checked the clock. It was two forty-five and I'd promised Kathy I'd be home by three. I raced back to her house, rushing into the Princess Suite, ripping off my clothes in an unprincess-like manner. Showered, dressed, and ready, I went upstairs to check on Kathy and, of course, she wasn't even close to being ready. While I had been trying to convince my aunt to stop searching for locks of Michael Jackson's hair, Kathy had gone for a hike. I guess after three days with me she needed some exercise.

She called me into her bedroom, where she needed help deciding on an outfit, something not too flashy but glamorous enough to distract from my frumpy corduroy blazer. She settled on a sweater-pants combo with a pink Valentino coat. Finally, I thought, we can get on the road to Nia's. Not so fast, we needed to bring gifts. Kathy—who doesn't drink—has a wine fridge filled with expensive bottles of champagne that people have given her as gifts. And, as my mother will tell you, there is no greater holiday joy than regifting. So Kathy and I took out two bottles of Dom Pérignon and slapped thank-you cards on them. Actually, "slapped" isn't entirely accurate. Kathy almost used an entire roll of tape securing the cards to the bottles. "If they don't know who it's from," she wisely explained, "it doesn't count."

By the time we got to Nia's house, we were at least forty-five minutes late, which is apparently gauche on Thanksgiving or, you know, always. We walked in and Kathy took the blame for our tardiness by announcing to a roomful of virtual strangers, "Hi, everyone, sorry we're late. Jack was masturbating." Which, sadly, is one of the better introductions I've had. Nia seated us and fed us and we became engrossed in the collective conversation, much of which had to do with competing corn breads being passed around the table. I don't eat corn bread and Kathy was basically like "they're both terrible," so our presence was so far a bit of a bust.

Meantime, I was trying to think of the name of the woman sitting across the table from us. She looked familiar, but I couldn't place her. Then Kathy asked, "Jewel, is that you?" It turned out the woman was the singer Jewel, who was there with her husband, Ty, a rodeo cowboy who had been on *Dancing with the Stars*. Ty was almost completely silent, scarcely saying a word. So, naturally, every few minutes Kathy would look over at him and say, "Shut up, Ty, I'm tired of your shit." For her part, Jewel would lean into his shoulder and quietly yodel.

Dinner was delicious. Nia and her husband, Ian Gomez, star of the show *Cougar Town,* served every dish you could imagine. And that was before dessert, which was so insanely good that I was still e-mailing Nia about it in the middle of the night months later. My e-mails included the words "pie" and "orgasm." Which might explain why she stopped writing me back. But the thing about dessert was that just as everyone was kind of stretching their legs and mingling, before migrating from the dining room into the kitchen, Jewel and Ty donned their jackets and announced they were leaving. They had to stop by another friend's house. Which would have been totally normal, by the way, if Jewel were not also holding a cake box, which contained the very cake she had brought with her. So, if we understood her correctly, she brought a cake to Nia's house for Thanksgiving and was leaving with the same exact cake.

For some reason no one else seemed to dwell on it, but Kathy and I were not letting it go. "Are we just going to pretend that didn't happen?" Kathy asked. "Did Jewel just take her fucking cake home?" No one seemed to know or care. But we were on a mission. It was like a pilot for a *Law & Order* spin-off airing on the Food Network. We got to the bottom of it. Jewel had been joking. She had not taken her own cake but rather a sugar-free pie that Nia was sure no one would eat. Oh, Jewel, that rascal. Basically she showed up at that next party with a fancy bakery box that everyone probably thought contained a decadent cake instead of the world's saddest sugar-free pie.

I had been telling Kathy and Nia for months that they should hang out. They both work in comedy and have similar senses of humor. It was only natural that they be friends. Going over to Soleil Moon Frye's house for dessert, however, was a different situation. Soleil is sweet and ethereal and Kathy is, well, Kathy. So when I told Soleil that Kathy was my Thanksgiving date, I half-expected that she would rescind her invitation. Instead she said she loved Kathy and had fond memories of going to watch her perform in the Groundlings, the L.A.-based comedy troupe. So, I felt relatively relaxed as we went there after leaving Nia's, aside from knowing that we were running late.

We sat down with the adults in the dining room, where dinner had just concluded. Soon, there were kids running around, hollering and dancing to music. It took all of fifteen seconds before Kathy—who does not like children—was rolling her eyes.

Soleil started handing out homemade Twinkies. I crossed my fingers.

On the way home that night, Kathy kept saying how she'd had fun but "what the fuck *was* that?" I had no idea, but I loved it.

The morning after Thanksgiving I had to return my rental car. Kathy offered to follow me down to the rental agency and drive me back, but I told her I'd either walk or take a taxi, both of which are unheard of in L.A. She wanted to have me tested for drugs. But I insisted, so after I dropped off the rental, I started walking up toward the Hollywood Hills like some sort of out-of-shape drifter in tube socks. I told myself that the exercise would do me good, which made sense in theory, but not when I was clinging to a guardrail as cars whizzed by at sixty miles per hour. By the time I made it back to Kathy's house, I had sweated out the equivalent of two pumpkin pies: one from exertion and one from fear. But there was no time to rest.

In a short while we would be headed to the airport to board a private jet for Las Vegas, where Kathy was performing at Caesars Palace the following night. This is not my life, I reminded myself, as I had many times before, this is Kathy's life. I must have been especially tired because I passed out as soon as I boarded the plane at Van Nuys. When I woke up, I looked out the window and saw a giant pyramid. I was so groggy that for a moment I thought maybe we were in Egypt, but the Caesars Palace limousine on the tarmac cleared that up.

I'd never been to Las Vegas before. I don't know why not. I think I just assumed that between the gambling and the debauchery, I'd end up going home in a body bag. But going with Kathy was different. She was treated like royalty. I was a high-roller by association. Unfortunately for Caesars, I had a gambling budget of roughly $5. I was just there to keep her company and to be a buffer between her and the countless foreign tourists who would just walk up to her with their cameras and start snapping, all the while saying, "I take picture, I take picture."

Saturday night was show night. As I sat backstage in the massive dressing room, I had one of those moments that I think everyone has from time to time. The kind of moment when you realize that life isn't what you expected it to be, and that the random times are some of the best times.

It was incredibly peaceful. And then, as I leaned back and shut my eyes, I heard a familiar voice say onstage, "I don't know what you guys did for Thanksgiving, but my fucking friend Jack dragged me to Soleil Moon Frye's house."

PIGEON IN A CROSSWALK

When I was little, my great-grandmother Nana would tell anyone who would listen—usually one of the many distant relatives whom she had targeted for a guilt trip—that she talked to her grandson by telephone every Sunday afternoon. She was proud of that, prouder still that she insisted they alternated who called whom. She'd be damned if staying in touch with family was going to be solely on her dime.

I always found it odd that Nana had such a regimented life that even a phone call had to be scheduled in advance. It made me sad. I would go over to her apartment with my grandfather to deliver her groceries, and she would be sitting in a chair, waiting for the phone to ring. And the calls were never long enough, nor were the in-person visits. It didn't matter how long you were there, you could camp out at her apartment and rub her bunions for a week. When you left, she'd still sigh and say, "Oh well, I guess you have more important things to do." In the car on the way home, my grandfather's assessment was always the same, "If I ever get that old, shoot me."

It was never my intention to be a once-a-week phone-call person. I called people when I had something to say, and when I didn't have anything to say, I didn't call. Then one day I woke up and I lived in New York City and I kind of had a life and I was sort of busy. I couldn't be bothered to answer a call, much less make one. It didn't take a long time for my mother to drop a hint or two in voicemails: "Hi, Jacky, I'm just calling to say hi and check in. No need to call me back." To know my mother is to know that "no need to call me back" is code for "please confirm you're not dead." So I started calling my mother once a week, usually on weekend afternoons, almost always when I was walking Sammy. Updating my family on my life while picking up dog shit feels right.

New York City's West Village is one of the city's most expensive neighborhoods for good reason, as far as reasons for New York real estate prices go. It's quaint, stylish, and chock-full of celebrities. I lived there for two years, in what one could call either a charming little studio or a tiny shithole. It was plenty of space, as long as you didn't want to have sex horizontally or vertically. But in terms of a neighborhood to walk my dog in, I couldn't have asked for anything better. The streets in that part of the city don't run on the traditional grid system. They wind and crisscross and altogether insist you pay attention, lest you end up lost on Sarah Jessica Parker's front steps. So I remember exactly where Sammy and I were walking on the afternoon my mother asked me, "What's that music in the background?"

"Carly Simon. Someone must have a window open," I said as we turned the corner from Barrow Street onto Commerce Street. A few yards up we turned another corner, as the street made an L-shape. I stopped. The music, it turned out, wasn't coming from someone playing a Carly Simon album with the window open; it was coming from Carly Simon, sitting on the sidewalk, singing and playing her guitar. She couldn't have been more than twenty feet away from me. "Oh. My. God. It's *Carly Simon*," I whispered into the phone. *"Shut UP!"* my mother said. *"You* shut up!" I said, "I'm not joking. Listen!" And then I proceeded to stand in front of Carly Simon, on a quiet West Village side street, holding up my cellphone like a lunatic. Unflappable, she kept right on going, singing, smiling, and strumming her guitar. I noticed a woman with two professional-looking cameras, discreetly taking photos of Ms. Simon for what must have been a magazine or promotional shoot. I didn't care. Even if it wasn't Carly Simon organically deciding to sing on the sidewalk, it was pretty close. I was spellbound. I don't remember what song she sang. I don't even remember hanging up the phone. What I do remember is applauding when she was done and rambling on to her about how amazing she was.

As I made a complete ass out of myself, Sammy—fed up with Carly Simon getting all of my attention and perhaps resentful of her marriage to James Taylor—took advantage of the slack in the leash to lunge. Not a threatening lunge, but a lunge nonetheless. My dog lunged. At Carly Simon. It happened in slow motion. I pulled back on the leash, but it was too late. Sammy had her tongue out and she went right for that guitar, scoring a giant lick before I pulled her away like the deranged, disrespectful-to-a-musical-icon embarrassment she was. My dog

just licked Carly Simon's guitar. I didn't know whether to yell at
her or swab her tongue for an eBay listing. Naturally, I did what
any Carly Simon fan would do. I got the hell out of there.

That wasn't Sammy's first celebrity encounter in New York.
She once tried to sniff Calvin Klein as he walked by. Really, can
you blame her? The West Village had proven to be an upgrade
in star sightings for Sammy. Before that, she and I had lived in
the Gramercy neighborhood on the East Side of Manhattan.
It was my first year in New York and I had wanted to bring
Sammy down from Boston with me right away. Unfortunately,
my new roommate had been incorrect when he told me that
yes, his building indeed allowed dogs. Apparently, I should have
asked to see such specifics in writing or at least asked him, "Are
you taking bong hits as you relay this information to me?" Because he didn't know what he was talking about.

It was printed right there in the lease, "No Pets." I was apo-
plectic. Technically, I hadn't signed anything, but I had already
given him all the money I had. Locked into a six-month sublet
with no way out, the nightmare scenario ran through my head:
I'm going to have to give Sammy up for adoption. Sobbing, I
called my mother in the middle of the night. It was a sad call,
although not as sad as a call I had made to her in the middle of
the night a few months earlier. I had called her up screaming at
2 A.M. that I was outside a Store 24 in Boston and had just won
$200,000 on an instant scratch lottery ticket. I was staring at the
ticket, sure of it. Sure of it until about ten seconds into the call,
when I realized that I had only won $20.

That I wasn't calling to tell her that I had lost Sammy on
some underground roulette wheel was a step in the right direction. My mom agreed to keep her for six months, a huge

commitment, even for a dog-lover. I thanked her and made a mental note to check the Web site of her local humane society regularly, just to make sure Sammy hadn't "accidentally" run away.

Six months goes by fast in New York. A few weekends at clubs, a few nights in the ice-cream section of Duane Reade, and, boom, I was ready for a new sublet. I found a place just a few blocks away that allowed dogs. It was a roommate situation, but the guy only lived there part-time, a huge plus. It was a beautiful apartment and way more than I should have been spending, but I was tired of searching for a place, so I scraped enough together for the first month's rent and hoped like hell I'd soon get a raise at work. After all, I'd been there for six months. I was due for a senior-vice-president title. The weekend after I moved in, my dad and grandfather drove Sammy down for our big reunion. Until then the longest she'd ever been in a car was forty-five minutes. After the five-hour trip to New York she was bouncing off the ceiling of my dad's Dodge Stratus, or whatever boring car he had that year.

Our life together resumed seamlessly. That is, until the first time she had to go outside to pee. Suddenly, I realized that maybe a fifth-floor walk-up wasn't such a great idea. Neither was my part-time roommate. He meant well and wasn't a dog-hater, but I don't think either of us fully considered what introducing a seventy-pound Labrador retriever into a theretofore spotless apartment would do for the living dynamic. Even though I knew Sammy and I would be moving when the sublet was up in six months, I did my best to get her acclimated to general city life. We established our short, medium, and long walking routes. The short one was just for inclement weather, days when I would stand on the corner wearing my knee-high plastic rainboots and an oversized t-shirt reading NO ONE KNOWS I'M A LESBIAN shouting, "Please, I'm begging you to poop. Please! Poop!" Fortunately our long route more than made up for those rainy days. It took us past the Carvel shop on Second Avenue. Apparently it is possible to gain weight during a three-mile walk.

Sammy may have been getting plenty of exercise, but she was getting ripped off as far as celebrity encounters went. Obviously, that's what dogs care about. The only celebrity we ever saw in that neighborhood was Paulina Porizkova, the former supermodel. She was a semiregular at the dog park. I didn't know who she was, and I was more fascinated by a woman at the park I referred to as Japanese Rosie O'Donnell. It was time to move.

It was Sammy's first experience with the paparazzi. As is her wont, she fucked it up. We were taking our evening walk up Bank Street past the Waverly Inn, the West Village hot spot owned by *Vanity Fair* editor Graydon Carter when two big SUVs pulled up right in front of us. Out of one jumped movie mogul Harvey Weinstein and out of the other jumped Puff Daddy, or P. Diddy, or whatever name Sean Combs was using that year. Diddy, or whoever, was wearing a fur coat. The two men embraced, bathed in the flashbulbs of photographers outside the restaurant. Reminding me once again that I'm too slow to hit the lock on the retractable leash, Sammy dashed toward the frenzy. Instead of gracefully posing like a respectable starlet, she weaseled in on someone else's photo op.

As if my dog trying to break up the Weinstein-Diddy power

couple wasn't bad enough, another experience walking past the Waverly Inn was even worse. We were minding our own business. Well, I was, God only knows what that sketchy dog was thinking. As we approached the corner, I could see there were a few paparazzi standing around outside the Waverly. Nothing big, I assumed. Wrong again. At the precise moment Sammy and I—she in her orange bandana, I in the sleeveless workout shirt that so beautifully showcased my nonmuscles— walked past the front door, it opened and the flashbulbs went off. Sammy, who rarely makes a sound, was spooked. And she barked. Not a cheerful, happy bark. A tense, what-the-fuck bark. "Whoah," the person coming out of the restaurant said, as he jumped back a step, startled by my nutbag of a dog. As I looked over and saw whom Sammy had just barked at, I could feel the blood drain from my face. "I'm so sorry," I told Steven Spielberg and his wife, Kate Capshaw. "That's OK," he said, "I'm used to being barked at." Maybe he was referring to his own dogs, or maybe his family, or perhaps Tom Hanks. Once again, we did not stick around.

From then on, I didn't walk Sammy past the Waverly Inn. It was embarrassing enough that I couldn't get a table there. I didn't need her peeing on Rihanna or trying to hump Anna Wintour. More than once I wished that I had a dog that was stable in public. I could have taken her to obedience school, but I didn't have the money. At least not after I paid for necessary monthly expenses like rent, electricity, and cookie cakes. Priorities, people.

I got my hopes up the day I ran into MSNBC's Rachel Maddow outside of my building. She lived in the building next door with her black lab. Finally, I thought, I've met someone who can relate to walking around a big dopey Labrador on the chic streets of the West Village. And not just anyone—a busy, sophisticated journalist like me. I introduced myself, mentioned that we had a mutual friend, and exchanged pleasantries for a minute or two. Of course, her dog was perfectly behaved while Sammy got tangled up in her own leash and chomped on a squirrel carcass.

For all the awkward encounters during our time in the Village, there were some smooth moments, too. Sammy got a "Hello, dog" from Julia Roberts as we "mistakenly" walked through the set of her movie *Duplicity*. And even though we never met her, I was proud that Sammy learned how to pee on cue outside of Gisele Bündchen's townhouse. Show me a dog from obedience school who can do *that*. But the razzle-dazzle is never enough of a reason to stick around, especially not in a studio apartment, especially not in New York, where there's always something going on, no matter where you live.

After two years downtown, we said goodbye and moved to the Upper West Side, where fun people go to become boring and NBC sitcoms go to shoot exteriors. For the first time since moving to New York in January of 2007, I felt like Sammy and I had a real home, an apartment where she would have enough space to walk around and I would have enough space to mourn the loss of feeling thin by association.

If the Upper West Side is dull compared to downtown, which it is, it also provides Sammy and I with a better quality of life. The streets are quieter. The sidewalks are cleaner. Our 3 A.M. walks are more relaxing, free from tourists and drunks, though not from rats. Those fuckers are everywhere. On weekends, unfortunately, uptown is filled with happy couples pushing strollers and towing long-forgotten golden retrievers. It's not that I'm opposed to relationships and procreation. What bothers me is the plodding, ubiquitous presence of countless New Yorkers—many of whom are my age or younger—who insist on walking around in real pants instead of pajama bottoms.

I don't have much in common with the textbook adults who crowd the Upper West Side. The weddings. The kids. Yawn. It's all I can do to get out of bed before 2 P.M. on Saturdays. I stumble out of my building wearing whatever I had on the night before, Sammy's leash in hand. We join the parade of New York families, ours no less important, no more important, than any other. Like my smiling neighbors pushing strollers, I am also trying to build a life for myself and a loved one. Sometimes it feels daunting. Work. Rent. Sammy's expenses. Figuring out what I want to do, what kind of life I want. Sometimes I wonder if I will eventually leave the city, defeated. One day I am especially stressed. Bills are due, I'm running late to work, and depression is weighing me down. Sammy and I are standing in a crosswalk, about to cross West End Avenue. I look down to my left and see a pigeon standing next to us. The light changes and the pigeon crosses the street, staying within the crosswalk the entire time. A pigeon. A pigeon! I'm losing sleep over whether I can get my shit together, whether I can sustain a life for myself in New York, and there's a fucking pigeon out here using the crosswalk. A pigeon that seems pretty happy with himself. I am clearly doing something wrong. At that moment I decide Sammy and I will be fine. If that bird can adapt and succeed in the big, complicated city, I can, too. The bar has been set by a pigeon in a crosswalk.

I've always struggled with the notion of putting my dog first. Should I adapt to her needs or vice versa? Sammy loves going to Central and Riverside Parks on the Upper West Side, but it's not like she knew what she was missing. And just because we are now in proximity to acres of green grass doesn't mean she can be trusted to go off-leash. The girl is a menace. She's never met a senior citizen whose crotch she didn't want to sniff, nor does she have any qualms about doing a modified *Free Willy* jump to snatch an ice-cream cone from the hands of an unsuspecting kid. And don't think she won't stick her head into a stroller to check for stray Cheerios or run off with someone's plastic sled in her mouth.

The only celebrity interaction Sammy gets uptown is our neighbor across the hall, an actor who has been in many successful movies and on a hit sitcom. He and his wife, also a well-known actor, smoke a lot of marijuana and watch a lot of game shows. Many nights Sammy and I inhale the smoke seeping out from their doorway as we wait for the elevator, listening to them shout out answers from *Jeopardy*. We have never been invited over for game night.

My friends used to ask me if I regretted bringing Sammy to live with me in New York. I guess they think it's an inconvenience when I have to leave the bar to go home and feed her, or battle a hangover to take her for a morning walk. And, yes, those are inconveniences, and, yes, I spend those walks telling her how I will soon take her to the pound. But she's part of my life. She's not an object, she's not a tenant. I don't have children,

I have no idea if I ever will. Sammy might be the closest I ever get to factoring someone else's comfort into my future. Maybe I'll be on the Upper West Side for decades, or maybe I'll move back downtown to reclaim my lost waist. I don't know where I'll end up. But I know that Sammy only cares about where her next meal is coming from. And I love that about her.

AUTHOR'S NOTE

Portions of some essays originated in blog form.

ACKNOWLEDGMENTS

This book would not have been possible without the support and encouragement of Anderson Cooper. I am immensely grateful for all he's done for me. It's a privilege to call him a mentor and a friend.

I am thankful to my outstanding agents, Luke Janklow and Claire Dippel, for having faith in me. Their steadfast backing and wise guidance are invaluable. What's more, they are wonderful people.

Ben Loehnen's tremendous skill as an editor is rivaled only by his kindness and good humor. He has my utmost gratitude. I would also like to thank Kate Gales, Jessica Abell, Brit Hvide, Fred Wiemer, Gypsy da Silva, Joel Holland, Jackie Seow, and Veronica Jordan for their exceptional efforts on this book's behalf, as well as Jonathan Karp and everyone at Simon & Schuster who decided to take a chance on me. I am deeply grateful to Kerri Kolen for championing me early on.

Charlie Moore's support has been essential, and I owe him a

great deal, personally and professionally. He is a peerless television producer and one hell of a guy.

Kirk McDonald, Makario Sarsozo, Jenny Blanco, Eliza Browning, and Dan Kloeffler have been unfailingly supportive. They have my love and appreciation.

Michael Hastings's advice and friendship have been crucial. I also thank Elise Jordan for her encouragement.

My thanks to Andy Cohen and Nia Vardalos for their friendship and kind assistance. Thanks as well to my dear pal Soleil Moon Frye.

Chet Curtis is one of my favorite people in the world. I am lucky to know him. I also thank Jim Braude, R.D. Sahl, Charlie Kravetz, Tom Melville, Phil Balboni, Bob Keating, Jan Saragoni, Geoff Gagnon, and Jared Bowen.

Kathy Griffin is a singular figure in my life. She brings fun and excitement wherever she goes, and I treasure every moment we've spent together. I'd also like to thank Justin Ongert, Whitney Tancred, and Tiffany Rinehart.

Kathleen Friery, Erica Hill, Randi Kaye, and Dr. Sanjay Gupta are friends whose enthusiasm and support have buoyed me at important moments.

Dave Cullen was generous with his time, and I thank him for his advice.

I am thankful to Brian Ulicky for his insight.

Scott Hornsby was kind enough to take my jacket photo. He's also a great friend.

I thank Bart Feder, Joey Gardner, Kara Kasarjian, Mary Anne Fox, Kerry Rubin, Sean Yates, Susan Chun, Tom Foreman, Shimrit Sheetrit, Marshall Arbitman, Jackie Puskas, Ella Chick, Alex Poolos, Barclay Palmer, Ted Fine, Jamie Kraft, David Doss, Penny

Manis, Jill Billante, Rebecca Sinderbrand, Liz Hayden, Samuel Burke, Eva Nordstrom, Jane Caplan, Jason Rovou, Geoff Doner, Anne Clifford, Elise Miller, Kira Kleaveland, Brittany Harris, and Alex Mooney for their encouragement and collegiality.

My love and special thanks to Mark, Alyssa, Lisa, Nicholas, Richie, Nick, Morwenna, Robby, Mat, T.J., and Liz.

Most of all, thanks to my family for their love and humor.

ABOUT THE AUTHOR

Jack Gray is an Emmy Award–winning producer for CNN's *Anderson Cooper 360°*. Born and raised in Massachusetts, he previously worked as a television producer in New Hampshire and Boston. He lives in New York City with his Labrador retriever, Sammy.